EMBODIED MEDITATION

"This is a clear-eyed, transformative guide that everyone can benefit from. With love and rigor, Karin van Maanen and Mark Walsh have synthesized the power of meditation when practised in an embodied way. The lessons in these pages clearly come from the author's experience, and so many people will benefit."
—David Treleaven, PhD, author of *Trauma-Sensitive Mindfulness: Practices for Safe and Transformative Healing*

"If attention isn't embodied, it isn't mindful attention. This innovative book makes this abundantly clear, as Walsh and Van Maanen bring their wealth of skill and experience in embodied arts, to teaching meditation practices grounded in and potentized by the sensory immediacy and somatic intelligence of bodily life."
—Martin Aylward, author of *Awake Where You Are: The art of embodied awareness.*

"Embodied Meditation is a clear and accessible guide written with care and the wish to benefit others. Dive in!"
—Emma Slade, Author of *Set Free*, Buddhist nun, Founder and Managing Director of Opening Your Heart To Bhutan.

"Meditation needs embodiment as much as embodiment needs meditation. No other resource has this many practical exercises for bridging these two worlds. If you are an embodiment practitioner who wants to deepen your meditation, or an established meditator who wants to integrate embodiment into your practice, then Mark & Karin's new book on 'Embodied Meditation' is for you!"
—Miles Kessler – Meditation Teacher, Aikido Sensei, & host of the "Meditate On This" podcast.

"Karin and Mark have written a remarkable book drawing on their experience and love of the embodiment journey. I found it an enjoyable and insightful guide for anyone involved in an embodied practice"
—Carole Moore, Mindfulness Facilitator and Aikido Teacher.

"A book on meditation that makes you laugh out loud? Yes, please! Embodied Meditation' is authoritative without being pompous, has a deliciously friendly tone and is full of great ideas for beginners and experienced practitioners alike. A refreshingly real and relatable meditation handbook which is encouraging, charming and full of wit."
—Bridget Hurst, Writer and Meditation Practitioner.

"It's a ballsy take on mindfulness and meditation practice with fantastic suggestions on embodiment meditations, I've learnt a lot from it."
—Yvonne Fuchs (Author, Creativity & Mindfulness Teacher and founder of the Zen of Business).

"There's no way I'm giving Mark a quote for the new book."
—Depak, California

"Seriously, this is the Shizzle."
—Prince Sid, India.

EMBODIED MEDITATION

MINDFULNESS, THE BODY, AND DAILY LIFE

BY

MARK WALSH AND KARIN VAN MAANEN

Unicorn Slayer Press

First published 2021, by Unicorn Slayer Press

© 2021 Mark Walsh

ISBN: 978-1-9162492-3-3 (pbk)
ISBN: 978-1-9162492-8-8 (ebk)

CONTENTS

CHAPTER 1   Theory   1

CHAPTER 2   Preliminaries   27

CHAPTER 3   Embodied meditation techniques   43

CHAPTER 4   Challenges and supports   103

CHAPTER 5   Over to you (establishing a practice)   111

CHAPTER 6   Conclusion and resources   121

ACKNOWLEDGEMENTS

Throughout this book, we've done our best to credit and thank all of those teachers and mentors who influenced the direction of the work presented here. Thanks also to Jane, Steve, Rosa, our team of social media volunteers and Karl for helping to put this book together, and Matt, Timi and Laurence for the wonderful graphics and photos contained herein.

Karin would also like to posthumously thank Jack Kerouac for initiating the desire to become a Dharma Bum in her. And all who have since accompanied and guided her in that quest.

Mark just says "cheers mate" to everyone. Because he's both cool and lazy . . . but is actually very grateful to all his long-tormented Dharma friends and teachers.

CHAPTER 1

THEORY

1.	WHO THIS BOOK IS FOR	1
2.	WHY INCLUDE THE BODY IN MEDITATION	2
3.	HOW THIS BOOK WORKS	11
4.	WHAT IS EMBODIED MEDITATION	13
5.	IN WHAT WAY TO PRACTISE EMBODIED MEDITATION	19

1. WHO THIS BOOK IS FOR

- People new to meditation who want a clear, practical and effective approach
- People for whom modern mindfulness with its bias of "MIND over body" has not been a good fit, and who want to try a different approach which includes the body
- Intermediate to advanced meditators who'd like to take an in-depth look at the bodily aspects of practice
- Movement arts practitioners (yogis, dancers, martial artists, etc.) who want a meditation book to better match their needs
- Anyone wanting a "Western and deep" approach to mindfulness, who wants neither a watered-down secular approach, nor to take on the cultural and religious (esoteric) trappings of Buddhism

- Anyone intuitively drawn to going deeper into their bodily experience
- Anyone "with" a body!

2. WHY INCLUDE THE BODY IN MEDITATION?

Context

Many of us are disconnected from our bodies. This leads to a sense of not feeling whole, being ill at ease, and often just being unhappy. Being cut off from ourselves also leads us to disconnect from others, resulting in everything from loneliness, to intimacy issues, to violence.

We ignore our bodies at our peril – pushing ourselves too hard, suppressing emotions, creating nervous system imbalances and losing sight of our bodies' innate wisdom. Critically, when we are distant from our primary "home", we lose touch not just with ourselves, but also with our values, other people (empathy is embodied), and the natural world. Embodied connection isn't just central to a healthy life, it is the essence of being alive, and what makes life worth living.

Many people have started practising mindfulness in recent years in a quest to remedy common modern ailments such as stress and anxiety, or to seek something deeper beyond modern consumer culture. As long-term meditators who have benefited hugely from the practice we celebrate this. And we have seen with some concern how the "mind" in "mindfulness" (incidentally only one translation of the original Pali word "*sati*") and distortions during the introduction of mindfulness into Western culture, has led to some serious misunderstandings. Things that were once perhaps a given now need clarifying and highlighting.

Times have also changed. Human beings are FAR more comfortable and sedentary than during the era of mindfulness' inception. In addition, the cultural transfer of Asian practices to a hyper-cognitive Western culture necessitates new explanations and techniques. As long-term movement practitioners we also know that dynamic conscious awareness practices and modern innovations,like trauma sensitivity, can inform traditional sitting meditation.

This book addresses these two concerns of distortion and the need for fresh adaptation with something both old and new. A lot of the traditional practices were more embodied than modern secular "mindfulness" and simply need restating and underlining. These can be combined with a new methodology for the age we live in, which incorporates fresh wisdom and also addresses current conditions such as the prevalence of technology.

A problem with modern meditation

Let us be blunt: most meditation as it is commonly taught does not encourage embodiment, but actually increases numbing and decreases body connection. It can easily be a tool for "spiritual bypassing" – trying to transcend the body, life and emotions. Meditation can lead people away from awareness of the body, or at least not optimise the benefits of a body-based practice. We believe that without an embodied "upgrade" as an option, meditation will do little good in the modern context, and can even cause harm.

Some of the traditional approaches are more helpful to embodiment than cognitive modern mindfulness approaches. Additionally, fresh perspectives and ways to meditate are very useful to explore for an embodied approach.

Beginners can start right away using the instructions in this book, while long-term practitioners, already working with the body, will find it helpful to focus on this aspect of practice. Both groups will be served by this book.

> *In short: Meditation needs to come home to the body to be kind and effective today, and this book is a guide on how to do that.*

Note too that the limits of embodiment which you can reach through meditation are FAR beyond what most people think possible. The myriad of benefits to an embodied approach, which we'll detail later in the book, include increased:

- Happiness
- Health
- Emotional intelligence (including empathy and self-regulation)
- Intuition
- Leadership impact and influence

Do not believe us, test it for yourself! Please never just believe us without experiencing it yourself. This is in fact one of the book's key principles[1].

The purpose of embodied meditation

> *Embodied meditation is the practice of being aware of what is happening in the present moment, as a body, with an attitude of kindness and acceptance.*

Awareness and choice

What does embodied meditation give you exactly?

Awareness practice is the core of embodiment. To be consciously embodied[2] is to be aware of yourself as a whole being. Not just your thoughts, not just your left knee that hurts, nor the fullness in your belly after a meal, but the whole of you. Being alive through a body.

Taking an embodied approach to the body means we experience the body not as an "it" (an object), but as part of ourselves. Embodied meditation is taking time to deliberately and skilfully reconnect in this way.

---

1 In line with a traditional empirical Buddhist approach, as it happens, too
2 We could also say everyone is unconsciously embodied, meaning they embody various attributes and have various habits of being

Embodied meditation will help you to build self-awareness, especially of those parts of "your" body, and therefore your being, which you don't normally notice. There are lots of things you are likely to discover that you don't normally notice during the course of your everyday life. Modern life is full of constant distractions away from our embodied selves, so it is helpful to have a dedicated practice of coming home again.

Once we understand that we do not just *have* a body, but that we *are* embodied, we realise that *our* body is not just a "brain taxi"[3] but is integral to *who* we are and *how* we live. Embodied meditation gives us more awareness of ourselves, and more choice in how we lead and develop ourselves[4].

Embodied meditation enhances our connection with the body, so we can make more skilful choices around how to be.

Embodied intelligence

One way of thinking about this book is as a guide to four skill-sets. These consist of awareness and influence, for oneself and others.

You can't change what you're not aware of, so we start here, with self-awareness. We will briefly cover the social domain in this book too.

Body awareness is a foundation of all embodied practice because whether you regulate or express yourself, or want to connect with or influence others, you need to start with what is already happening! While this entire book is concerned with the top left quadrant of the wider embodied intelligence model below, it is also the foundation of the other three.

---

3   Credit to Francis Briers for this expression.
4   This second "choice" part here could be seen as a departure from mindfulness as it's often practised as "just" non-judgmental awareness. And we would like to point out that Buddhist practise was always meant to be transformative, and practises to "cultivate" qualities like kindness in the short and long-term always existed in various traditions.

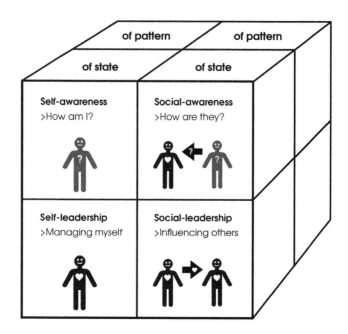

Embodied Intelligence

Why is it useful to know yourself as a body?

Aside from the fundamental re-humanising nature of coming back to yourself, once you know how you are, you can then make more informed decisions as to your state, and what you would like to eventually become. You cannot change what you are not aware of.

This is an ongoing process. Human beings continually change. The body is a verb. Nothing about your body is permanent. You interact with the world and other people, you learn, you celebrate, you love, you grieve, you achieve. We lay down new patterns of being based on trauma, relationships, how we live, where we live . . . all experience, in fact. Hence our embodiment shifts. Whether you are consciously practising something or not, you are always practising becoming something.

As creatures easily lost to abstract thought and distraction, we are just as easily disconnected from the body. We may not even know we are disembodied. In any event, it is necessary to come back to the body time and time again – hopefully connecting a bit more deeply each time.

The purpose of embodied meditation is not abstract spirituality. It's about being able to lead a more embodied life with increased awareness and choice. This is an effective doorway to freedom, happiness and connection.

Other kinds of meditation

There are many potentially useful practices that for example are focused on mindfulness of thoughts, visualisation techniques, or a small part of the body (like concentration on the breath at the tip of the nose). These approaches may be very useful, for instance as part of cognitive behavioural therapy which requires mindfulness of thoughts, or if you are training yourself to improve your concentration skills. These approaches are not the focus here. They may even be accidentally dissociative, despite not having this intention (and having some very positive potential benefits too).

If you are trained in such methods, this book can helpfully add to them as a support or further development, as there's no inherent contradiction. You will find that practising embodied meditation offers you a way to deepen some of these related practices, or will provide new options. They likely make a good foundation for what we'll present.

Meditation can also be practised as a way to "transcend" the body when it is seen as dirty, not spiritual, or something to overcome. Such actively anti-body approaches are in our opinion deeply harmful, and are far less compatible with this book. You may have a difficult choice if you have been formally trained in such an attitude.

The disembodied cultural context

Technical disembodiment and religious body repression aside, a "cogno-centric" attitude exists in most places today. Valuing abstracted reason over the body is an unquestioned cultural bias, and is likely to unhelpfully influence any meditation practice you take on. When schools have important "heads", football teams "captains" and we say "on the up" to mean improving, perhaps it is no wonder we all carry an implicit Cartesian bias. We have all been raised in an ideology of disconnection and if unquestioned, we will very likely bring this to anything we learn – including meditation[5]. Embodied meditation is therefore a kind of unlearning, especially for those of us from The West, despite its achievements.

Relationship to movement practices

Happily, awareness-based movement practices like yoga, martial arts, western somatic disciplines and conscious dance are becoming increasingly popular. Similarly, many people enjoy feeling their bodies through sports, outdoor activities and so on.

Lovers of such arts will no doubt get a lot from this book. We would suggest a greater level of sensitivity can be gained from the simple and still practices herein, which are complementary to more complex or athletic pursuits. We have both had our movement disciplines hugely enhanced by sitting practices over the years. There's a reason why traditionally many aikidoka or yogis also sat in meditation.

While "movement meditation" is on one level accurate to describe conscious movement arts, there is much to be gained from additional embodied meditation as described here. As well as increasing sensitivity, this book may lead to additional transfer to daily life, as it doesn't rely upon music, unusual positions nor intensity. Yoga and skiing are great for example, but it's hard to throw a cheeky

5   See Philip Shepherd's excellent work on this

downward dog pose into a business meeting for increasing calm, or demand your kids hurtle down a mountain with you when you want to feel connected. It's all great, all complementary, and everything is not the same.

General benefits of meditation vs enlightenment

Developing your capacity to be present in the here and now through meditation has many well-documented benefits. It can help increase focus, calmness, awareness of what is happening inside you and around you as well as make you more attentive to how you are and more (self-)compassionate. It can improve resilience, boost your immune system, and break the cycle of mild recurring depression. Of course, these will make a difference to your life already. All of these benefits have been widely researched and confirmed by mindfulness teachers and researchers such as Jon Kabat-Zinn at the Massachusetts Institute of Technology (MIT) and Mark Williams at Oxford University. They both pioneered research programmes, in the US and the UK respectively, which to this day inform many mindfulness-based stress reduction programmes available in healthcare, community and educational settings.

These now commonly known benefits of meditation are the "lower end" of what is possible. Lasting and impactful shifts in both perception and identity (i.e., various stages of "enlightenment") are possible with sustained practice, in turn dramatically reducing suffering and increasing capacity. Sadly, modern mindfulness tends to brush the upper reaches under the carpet. For many simply being able to concentrate better or be less stressed is a huge win, and we think it's wise to know much more is possible. We have not written this book as a guide to enlightenment; instead, we have more modest aims. What matters to us is an approach suitable for most people and for the real world.

That being said, The Buddha probably wasn't a complete idiot when he made something as bodily as breath central to his approach.

We also support the likes of Daniel Ingram who are removing the taboo around discussion of enlightenment, and strongly suspect an embodied approach will be helpful for many with this aim. Rather than skipping over the body, we are in agreement with many more realised masters of meditation, that including the body is hugely important for even those with the loftiest goals. While we do not claim more than temporary state experiences as personal attainments, we are assured by people we trust that "full awakening" is a deeply bodily matter and not about floating away with the angels.

An "ascending" or "descending" path?

Spiritual traditions have been categorised by philosopher Ken Wilber either as "ascending" or "descending", aiming us towards the one transcendent absolute, or towards the down-to-earth plurality. Towards the abstract or the manifest. *Via negativa* vs *via positiva* in theological terms. To deny the incarnate and the world, or to embrace it fully. To be a monk or a layperson with a family and a business. To fast and rise above your hunger, or enjoy the cake and your appetite for more food.

While we regard both paths as positive and having merit, and possible to integrate to some degree, an embodied practice is very much a "descending" path. What could be more "right here and now" than one's own body?![6]

In times where many of us cannot and will not give up "the world", perhaps an embodied approach, as opposed to some half-hearted impersonation of a renunciate, is highly appropriate. Or perhaps it could add balance to mainstream body-repressing religions, dissociative technology, distracting consumerism, and transcendent new age "love and light" approaches?

Personally, we like having our cake and meditating on it too.

---

6   This aligns with "tantric" approaches in Buddhist and Hindu traditions

3. HOW THIS BOOK WORKS

Our intention here is to offer you:

- A fresh and clarified perspective on the body in meditation
- Inspiration as to the importance of the body in meditation
- Practical tools and techniques suitable for complete beginners
- A guide to establishing a regular embodied meditation practice
- Help with common challenges that tend to crop up when meditating
- An effective way to integrate body awareness into daily life "off the cushion"
- "Advanced" tools and techniques suitable for experienced practitioners
- Further signposts and resources for those who wish to go deeper

Practise not faith

Never believe a word we say, find out if what we say is true by trying it out for yourself.

Critically, we are not asking you to take on a faith, nor a single style of meditation, but hope you will learn things that you can apply to whatever you do now. No belief is required to try what is here, and the work fits with almost any practice framework or belief system you may already value. We are both highly influenced by (different schools of) Buddhism, but it is not necessary to become a Buddhist to get anything from this book.

As we work with many kinds of students worldwide, it is important to us that people of any or no religion will find this book accessible.

So, if this book doesn't work through belief, then what? Through practice – this is the "trying it out". While people may read books to learn *about* something, this book is very much about learning *to do* something: embodied meditation. You will get most benefit if you not only do the exercises, but develop a regular practice with them. In fact, there is a chapter on how to do this, as it is so critical.

A bespoke "no guru" approach

We find that a "one approach fits all" solution does not work, so you will need to work creatively with us to design your own solution. We do not believe teachers should be like gurus telling you exactly what to practise, but rather more like waiters helping you make a good choice for where you are in your life and practice. The bad news is this requires some work and you won't get exactly what you need on a platter. The good news is you can find an individualised way that really works for you, using principles that will save you a lot of time compared to just trial and error.

How long will a shift take?

You may have been practising mindfulness of the body quite a lot, or you may be new to this altogether. It might take a while to develop your awareness as a body, and that's okay. For many of us, it means undoing habits of a lifetime. Practising is what it's all about. The embodied meditation method we present here offers a non-esoteric concrete skill set to achieve this.

The practices in this book are very, very likely to give you pleasant and useful state shifts immediately, but it takes longer to impact the level of your default "trait" mode. It is, however, a near guarantee that a modest daily practice will lead to major changes that people you care about will notice, and usually appreciate, within 2-3 months. It might not make you rich nor help you meet the person of your dreams, but it will positively impact your health, relationships and work.

4. WHAT IS EMBODIED MEDITATION?

Embodied meditation is:

- Meditating AS a body
- Coming home to the body
- Inhabiting oneself

- Self-intimacy
- Learning a very particular skill set

To "come home to the body" is an evocative and poetic phrase that summarises embodied meditation, and we find it resonates with many students, but what exactly do we mean by this? Well, we can think of it as a concrete skill set. It is paying more attention as a body, in a way that is:

- Complete (the whole body)
- Consistent (more of the time)

- Detailed (more subtlety)
- Deep (to more profundity)

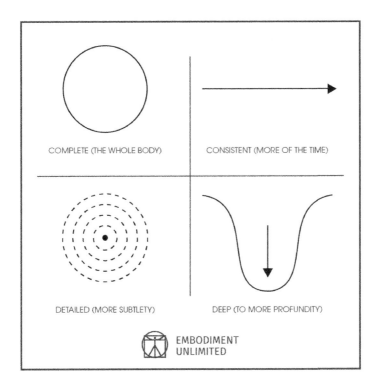

COMPLETE (THE WHOLE BODY)

CONSISTENT (MORE OF THE TIME)

DETAILED (MORE SUBTLETY)

DEEP (TO MORE PROFUNDITY)

EMBODIMENT UNLIMITED

To expand, embodied meditation is a journey into feeling the body in increased:

- *Completeness*
  Being aware of your whole body – not just bits of it (NB: this includes sensing deeper into your body than just the skin).

- *Consistency*
  Being aware of your body more of the time.

- *Detail*
  Sensing the subtleties of embodied experience. Greater sensory acuity.

- *Depth*
  The level of intimacy with bodily sensations.

  Our promise therefore is this: embodied meditation will make you aware of more of the body, in greater detail, more of the time, to a greater depth.

We could add that to do this necessitates decreased reactivity to the body, so the journey is also one of greater equanimity; and increased acceptance and inclusivity, so the journey is also one of love.

A reflection

Which of these is more accurate?

What would be the consequences of having each as a frame?

Which is the default perspective of any meditation you may have done previously?

- *Meditating DESPITE the body*
- *Meditating on YOUR body?*

- *Meditating on THE body?*
- *Meditating WITH the body?*
- *Meditating THROUGH the body?*
- *Meditating AS a body?*

These perspectives are profoundly different and lead to profoundly different outcomes, and they are often implicit. Listen out for their influence.

Aware AS a body, not just OF the body

Now a critical distinction from how mindfulness is usually "done".

> **We define an embodied approach to meditation as being aware AS a body not just OF the body.**

This means you are not an abstracted distanced observer looking dispassionately at your body from afar when you enter into embodied meditation. While we may sometimes say it's something you "do", "enter into" is more accurate. One practises inhabiting the body, as embodied meditation teacher Philip Shepherd says. Note that we try to avoid "my body" and "your body" as we do not predispose a separation, though as this is so common in daily language it can at times be awkward to never use it.

This difference between *"as a body"* and *"of the body"* concerns identity and separation. This may sound like a subtle distinction, but it is not. It is as different as thinking you are your t-shirt, from knowing you have one (but the other way around).

Things are tricky when a disembodied perspective is commonly the linguistic norm!

Our approach is actually quite traditional when one looks deeply into the Pali canon (early Buddhist texts) which, to take two decent translations of critical lines, talk of "womb-like" awareness and "feeling the body as the body". See our friend and colleague

Martin Aylward's book: *Awake Where You Are: The Art of Embodied Awareness*, or Christopher Wallis' *Tantra Illuminated* for more on this. These books are excellent complements to this one.

"Mindfulness" vs "Kindfulness", "Heartfulness" and "Bodyfulness"?

"Mindfulness" (or "*sati*") is often used synonymously with meditation. Mindfulness is, in fact, the capacity to be present during meditation, to remember to keep coming back to the present moment and what is happening there when we've become lost in distraction. We may have become disconnected from the here and now by daydreaming, or planning the future or analysing the past, for example. In that case, we have probably lost awareness of our body and our capacity to be aware as a body.

Most definitions of mindfulness include something about being non-judgmental, kind or accepting towards what is happening in the present moment and in the body. This is an inherent and important part of mindfulness practice and we will say more about that later.

Mindfulness of the body is the practice of remembering to come back to the body in the present moment. Being in the body in the present moment is a cornerstone of all embodied practice.

> *Embodied meditation then is the practice of being aware of what is happening in the present moment, AS A BODY, with an attitude of kindness and acceptance.*

That last part is key to what embodied meditation is, and is not just a "nice to have" extra. The attitude is the practice, far more so than the technique (e.g., scanning the body).

"Bodyfulness" is a term I (Mark) and another embodiment teacher started using independently a few years back to de-emphasise the "mind" part. "Heartfulness" is sometimes used today too. "Mind" and "heart" are actually combined as only one word in a number of Asian languages. While we find both heartfulness and bodyfulness a bit clumsy as words, they can be useful to point people to the bias in the term "mindfulness" and encourage a different approach.

A few words of caution

Whilst meditation is helpful for most people, it is not always great for everyone, all of the time. This is as true of embodied approaches as it is of others.

We recommend finding a qualified teacher/community to learn meditation from. A book like this can teach a lot, but over time you will definitely need support. As one's practice develops, it is extremely likely that some moderate to severe challenges will arise and, for many, disruptive psychological issues might come up, too (see Daniel Ingram or Willoughby Britton for more). Sometimes these are unpleasant, sometimes not, either way they can still make life hard to manage. I (Mark) once had a two-month period after a retreat where my entire body felt like effervescent-warm-bubbly-champagne love. Nice, but it did make doing my taxes hard.

In addition, if you are presently experiencing moderate to severe mental health issues, you may need a particular approach to meditation for it to serve you well and not harm you. Take extra care with more severe anxiety or depression, if you are traumatised or have PTSD. We recommend some resources at the end of this book, including David Treleaven's excellent work on trauma-sensitive mindfulness.

And if you are new to meditation and you have recently gone through a major life change such as a bereavement, divorce, redundancy, it may or may not be a good idea to delay starting your practice. This is where talking to a guide comes in handy.

More on Kindness

As stated previously, most definitions of mindfulness include something about being non-judgmental, kind or accepting. It is the heart of the practice – but doesn't always come naturally. This is an extremely common experience, so please don't judge yourself for being judgmental! Often when we slow down and start paying attention, such patterns become more obvious.

Some practices specifically focus on developing kindness and compassion. You may have heard of "metta" practice – a word from yoga and Buddhism which is often called "loving kindness" in English, but may be better translated as "universal / boundless friendliness". Developing an attitude of kindness is inherent in mindfulness practice. For most of us, it is part of what we need to practise, especially in regard to how we relate to ourselves. Many of us are not particularly kind nor even polite towards ourselves. Because of the practice, meditation practitioners often report they become aware that they are much less kind to themselves than they are to others. More critical for example, or more judgmental. When I (Karin) embarked on my meditation practice, I noticed how internally I was speaking to myself in a way I would not do to anyone else, and wouldn't accept from anyone else – calling myself a "stupid idiot" very regularly, for example.

Paul Linden, in his explorations of embodied peacemaking says we can "do love" with our bodies. When including an intention to develop loving kindness in our embodied meditation practice, we are not just thinking about it, or automatically repeating the type of well-wishing phrases typically used in a metta practice, such as: "May you be happy, may you be healthy". We can actually practise being more compassionate as a body in our meditation when we realise intentions can be embodied.

Developing attitudes of kindness and compassion are not about paying lip service to what we think is right, nor are they "to do" lists to tick off. Embodying kindness or recognising kindness as an embodied state may seem difficult for you. Again, this is very normal[7]. Your capacity for this depends on how much you have practised, and on how you are in your life – it will be harder to embody this when you're grumpy on a Monday morning after a poor night's sleep, for example. As you develop more of the depth and detail of awareness

7   One of my (Karin's) teachers, Tsoknyi Rinpoche, says you may have to fake it till you make it, and that's okay – we can at least develop the intention to be kinder and go from there.

mentioned earlier you will get a felt sense of this and will understand and increase your capacity to "do love".

Many insights can arise from practising mindfulness. We become more intimate with how we create our own reality and what we're doing with our bodies as well as our thoughts to create that reality. Knowing that,on an embodied level, opens the door to choice. And the addition of the balm of loving kindness can promote healing in itself. It has been well documented by researchers like Barbara Frederickson that developing a kind curiosity within the practice is part of how meditation can transform old patterns of thoughts and behaviour.

Lastly, we say that kindness is so integral to embodied meditation that we have a kind of catchphrase:

if it isn't kind, it isn't meditation.

It's a bit blunt but that's how we sit.

5. IN WHAT WAY TO PRACTISE EMBODIED MEDITATION

So far we've offered quite a few ideas as to what embodied meditation is, what it is not, and how it can improve your life. Hopefully you are motivated to put it into practise.

This chapter is an overview of the general theory of practice. Chapter Two is the preparation before trying out the techniques themselves in Chapter Three. Chapter Four looks at the issues that may come up and in Chapter Five we look at how to pick exactly what to do and establish your own routine.

In chapter 1

Formal vs informal vs applied

You may have heard about formal and informal meditation, or mindfulness on the meditation cushion and mindfulness in daily life. What is the difference?

Formal practice is what we reserve the term "meditation" for. It is completely dedicated, non-consequential and calibrated. This means its only purpose is to develop embodied awareness (in this case), it can be optimised for best results, and if you get it wrong you don't lose much (e.g., your life or your job). Its intention is to develop a skill. Note the intention is not to change your state, although this may well be part of what you do.

It's practised whilst sitting, standing or lying still, or in some schools of meditation, whilst walking slowly. This is what we call a formal meditation practice. We reduce activity and stimuli, which gives us the best chance to develop a deeper and more fundamental awareness of ourselves. We may practise alone, or together with others, in a place where distractions are less likely. We practise in silence, choosing a posture that helps us to stay awake and comfortable in our body. We practise for a certain amount of time – for example, ten minutes per day for beginners, to more than one hour per day for some people.

Informal practice refers to mindfulness in daily life, in contexts where conditions are simple and non-consequential enough. These conditions mean that enough of our attention is available for the

technique, as the task is not demanding. For example, when doing the washing up, brushing your teeth or driving a familiar route. There is still an intention to develop a skill.

This type of practice encourages transfer from formal practice into the rest of our life and enables us to "get the reps in", as most of us cannot dedicate too much time to formal practice.

Application refers to using mindfulness skills when you need them in your everyday life. For example, when you're arguing with your partner, when parenting, or within a business meeting. Here you are not so much focusing on developing a skill, but applying it to get a desired outcome.

For most of us application is the point of practice, but is not practice in itself.

This might sound like splitting hairs, but all three categories are very useful AND NOT THE SAME. It is very important to know that the formal practice informs the informal practice, and leads to skills that can be applied. It tends to be harder to be mindful amongst the distractions and pressures of our daily life, especially when in relationship with others, under stress or when using technology. We need to keep coming back to formal meditation to support the application of mindfulness in daily life. This is also why many meditation retreats promote silence or limited conversation between participants. Such conditions are ideal for practice.

These three categories are not the same. You will not develop much without a formal practice, as it enables you to develop skills such as greater clarity. And you cannot tell your kids to be 30% less annoying so you can continually stay in your practice "sweet spot"! Equally, if you just sit on a cushion and never make use of it in an applied way, what's the point?

We encourage people to develop skills and insights in a formal practice and apply these in their lives. If you practise walking meditation at home for example, you might then decide to walk to the shop more mindfully to transfer the skill into your life (only if you know the way and don't get run over). Or you can apply it so you can enjoy your walks more or get lost less often!

You might take the opportunity to informally practise in a queue, or to *apply* some mindfulness of breathing whilst waiting in line instead of getting impatient. You might bring more awareness to your senses whilst gardening as an informal practice, or choose to be fully present whilst listening to a friend talking about what is going on in their life to allow for a deeper connection (application).

The challenge is that limiting the factors of normal life (removing kids, talking, and consequences) increases ease and depth in formal practice, but reduces life transfer by making the conditions unrealistically simple. People can get good at something "on the cushion" but then not be able to use this where they really need it.[8] In the chaotic milieu of life application on the other hand, conditions are often too challenging for learning as you are trying to "perform". Informal practice is a good bridge between the two.

Another way of thinking about this is that practice puts mindfulness in the "bank", which we "spend" under pressure.

The four positions, and six conditions

We recommend practising the traditional four positions of formal meditation, as most of life is done in a variation of one of these: sitting, standing, lying down and walking. Some variety will lead to more transfer across life, e.g., sitting relates more easily to driving, standing to jobs like bar work, lying down to resting, etc.

Each can also be used to regulate your state for ideal internal conditions of meditation which we will outline later.

---

8 A classic example from one of Karin's teachers, Maarten Vermaasse, is the story of the monk who thought he had achieved total equanimity, if not enlightenment, by the end of a three-year retreat. He realises he has not when during his first meal "out", he ends up angrily shouting at a fellow monk for spilling some soup.

In addition to this traditional list, we would also recommend some kind of practice in each of these conditions:

- In nature
- With others in community (in silence)
- With stress/pressure (with a gradient from little to lots)
- With grasping/pleasure (with a gradient from little to lots)
- Verbal social communication
- Online/with technology

The idea of gradients means staying in the "sweet spot" of challenge but not overwhelm, and moving this forward with practice.

These are listed from easiest to hardest (for most people). So don't be surprised or judge yourself if being body aware in the park while meditating with a friend is easy and staying present during an online social media argument is hard!

Pit stops

In addition to formal sitting (or standing, lying or mindfully walking) for a period of time, it can be very helpful for life-transfer to practise embodied awareness for one minute, several times a day, "peppering" the practice throughout your life. You can set a mindfulness reminder on your phone or link this intention to recurring actions in your day; for example, each time you go to the toilet, make a phone call or walk through a door. For one minute, pay attention to how you are in your body right now. We call these "pit stops" because modern life can feel like being a race car. They are brief but deeply restorative for many and also help with integration.

Don't be fooled by the minimal time spent, or simplicity here, we have heard many seasoned sitters be surprised at their power. The very minimal time and energy commitment can enhance your general capacity to be embodied and present. We are big believers in "training smart, not hard" – conditions have changed considerably since most yogic and Buddhist paths were developed.

Why "just sit" versus yoga, conscious dance or mindful movement?

When you "just sit", you can discover a lot of things you are unlikely to notice in the midst of stimulation from movement, techniques, music, instructions from someone else etc. Subtle (and not so subtle) attitudes, thoughts, emotions and sensations in your body can be revealed in the stillness and the silence.

There is much to be gained from learning to do nothing. Not having the usual "crutches" of distraction, such as trailing through social media, listening to music or staying busy,can help you take a deeper look at how you really are, emotionally digest things (see below) and give considerable insight into yourself.

The simplicity of a stillness practice further helps you to prepare for taking this information and your capacity for mindfulness into your life – with all its potential complexity and distractions.

Skiing, spanking and drugging

Well, this sounds like a good weekend, right?!! But here's the point: there are many body practices from yoga to kink which bring people's attention back to the body with intense stimuli. Being licked or whipped is a very strong "crutch" as it will grab attention. Such things will take your attention with far less effort than simply sitting quietly noticing your breath, and may be very pleasant too, but are also:

1. Potentially addictive producing further numbing when the stimuli is not present, and requiring greater and greater stimuli to feel
2. Not that helpful for life transfer where the stimuli isn't present (you're reliant on the crutch, not developing a transferable skill)

Similarly, activities that require special conditions and equipment like skiing or diving, may well induce a pleasant altered flow state, but this is hard to transfer.

While we are not against hardcore hot yoga, rigorous dancing to hardcore trance music, intense martial arts, a damn good spanking or anything else consensual, these two points should be considered. Activities such as these do not replace traditional practice, even if they seem easier and more fun!

Drugs of course are also popular, but again are reliant upon external stimuli, and build neither lasting traits (as opposed to states) nor transferable life skills.

On a positive note, such things can give an example of a state which creates a reference point to head towards on one's own. They may be great for those who cannot yet bear to be still, as "gateway drugs" and supplementary activities to meditation.

Emotional digestion - another goal of embodied meditation

In addition to the goal of developing the four embodied awareness skills mentioned before (CCDD – Completeness, Consistency, Detail and Depth of awareness), we can also meditate as a body to help us "digest" experiences for emotional wellbeing.

Being with your emotions in the present moment with curiosity and kindness can be a significant and potentially healing part of the practice, as long as this is done in a way that doesn't lead to overwhelm (see the chapter on potential difficulties in the practice and trauma sensitivity).

We each have our own ways of dealing with emotional difficulties in daily life. This might involve ignoring or suppressing emotion by trying not to think about it or feel it, and escaping into some kind of distraction. This can result in addictive behaviours such as using social media, alcohol or being busy all the time in order to ignore uncomfortable feelings. In fact, I (Karin) realised at one point that I was using my yoga and meditation in this way. Because I got very good at calming myself down, I was able to escape from and ignore feelings that needed to be able to be felt and expressed in some way.

These tactics can lead us into a disembodied state – no longer connected to how we really are. Or we might engage in excessive thinking or talking about the issue, worrying, catastrophising in our mind. What tends to happen in all of these cases is that we actually bring more energy to the emotions we're trying so hard to avoid or resolve. Suppression and ignoring could be compared to holding a football under water – it takes a fair amount of effort and in the end, when we let go, the ball will come up anyway. Not only that, but the force we used to push and hold it under will be equivalent to the force that's released when it comes up. And excessive attention on an issue is like fanning the flames of a fire. It will get bigger and bigger and potentially out of control.

During meditation, the way to practise being with our emotions is to allow without intervening. To notice how emotion is felt in the body with kindness and curiosity. This allows emotions to be processed and move through you.

CHAPTER 2

PRELIMINARIES

"STANCE" - OUR FUNDAMENTAL ATTITUDES OF EMBODIED MEDITATION

A critical factor for success in meditation is one's "stance", or attitude. We like both words as they are extremely bodily. Dancers and sword fighters have stance and attitude, and they convey the congruence between our physicality and overall approach to meditation. Similarly, the word "posture" conveys emotional overtones in English, but we reserve this word for discussing body position to avoid confusion. An embodied perspective however is that there is never "just" a body position, or a mere mental "stance", as mind and body are intimately linked.

As with kindness, the subtle or gross "how" of meditation – its stance – is in many ways more significant than the "what" of the technique (more on this to come).

Distance and engagement

One has to resort to metaphors when describing differences in meditation stance, due to their potential elusiveness. This could become an intricate subject but there are two related critical factors that can be played with: how "close" one chooses to be to sensation, and how "involved" with it.

Here are some examples of this way of being with ourselves that will illustrate this:

- Sitting lovingly with a grieving friend (close and engaged)
- Holding a child's or old lady's hand (close and engaged)
- Witnessing[9] friends getting married (far and engaged)
- Lovingly keeping an eye on kids playing from a distance – making sure they're OK but letting them do their own thing (far and engaged)

As opposed to:

- Watching someone in the distance you have no connection to (far and disengaged)
- Hearing a voice in the background speaking a language you don't understand (far and disengaged)
- Reading numbers on a page that mean nothing to you (close and disengaged)
- The feeling of an unavoidable touch of a stranger's leg on yours, while sitting next to someone on a train or bus (close and disengaged)

Note that while more or less distance can be helpful (e.g., giving some space to difficult emotions), an embodied approach is also involved and never completely dispassionate. While we encourage a "witnessing" which distances oneself from thoughts and feelings, as per traditional meditation practice, we do not think that the notion of a detached observer is helpful for most people. Hence the colourful examples here. When you watch a wedding of loved ones you are intimately involved, though not interfering nor clingy. You still care.

---

9   Note "witnessing" is often used by meditation teachers and while this is not bad, it does have a certain "far" flavour

You are still connected. You wish them well (metta), but aren't going to join in the kiss.

This "stance" can be slippery. Don't worry if it doesn't make sense yet if you are only starting out. For intermediate and advanced practitioners however, we have found it incredibly valuable, and we recommend it as a major area to focus on.

The "how" IS the "what" at the end of the day.

EMBODIED MEDITATION POSTURES

The word "sitting" is often used as synonymous to meditating. However, as we referred to above, you can also meditate standing, lying down or whilst walking mindfully. Each of these approaches has a different effect on your embodiment (especially in terms of the balance between wakefulness and relaxation) and may be useful under certain circumstances. Each posture "translates" better to different actions in life (which we do in different positions), as mentioned previously.

We encourage you to try them out for yourself. Personal preference is a factor here, but do use a mix. While we don't go so far as to do them all equally and it being fine to have a favourite, it is helpful for life transfer to practise in each position from time to time, so they're all familiar for when your circumstances change. For example, we find standing is great when in a place with a dirty floor or no cushions, or when meditating late at night and feeling sleepy; and lying down when ill or agitated by some unusual stress.

A core postural principle

Find a position where you can balance wakefulness with relaxation; alertness with ease. Find the optimum combination, or sometimes "trade off", between these two conditions which are both necessary for meditation.

The main function of any posture in meditation is to foster the right balance of wakefulness and relaxation. Which of the four poses one chooses, and how one does it (e.g., slow or fast walking, bolt upright or more relaxed sitting), should be led by that balance. For instance, you can deliberately slump while sitting, or sit up "straighter" than would be wise long-term to wake up for a few minutes.

There is no "right" posture, but there are better postures for certain things; going to sleep can be accomplished standing up, but is much easier lying down. Postural adjustments take this common-sense idea and refine it.

You should adjust the macro level of which of the basic four postures to use when choosing how to meditate generally, and the micro level at any given moment of how exactly to do that posture if you'd like to stay in an optimal state. This latter subtle adjustment could be compared to tuning-in an old analogue radio, or adjusting a guitar string so it's not too tight or loose. For example, when practising standing or seated meditation, you can fine-tune being upright, balanced and alert as well as relaxed and at ease.

Sitting

Seated meditation is commonly practised in all meditation traditions, including the modern secular approach to mindfulness. It offers a certain amount of ease and stability, whilst promoting wakefulness. Traditionally, yogis would meditate sitting on the floor, cross-legged or in yoga postures like the lotus pose. The full lotus posture is not comfortable nor recommended for most people as it can be damaging to the knees. Whilst it can be very helpful to learn to sit on the floor – it may give you a sense of connection to the ground which is calming – it is not essential, and many people, including advanced meditators, use chairs or benches. The floor is not more spiritual.

The main thing is that you are comfortable enough so that discomfort or pain in your body does not become a major distraction. If you are experiencing pain or discomfort as a result of something else, you may need to learn to sit with it. It is unnecessary to create

more discomfort or hurt yourself for the glory of a pose! Practising on a chair can be useful sometimes, allowing your practice to transfer more easily to different circumstances in your daily life.

TIPS FOR SEATED MEDITATION

Use a chair if you cannot get comfortable on the floor. Sit upright on the chair so that you can feel your sitting bones and the soles of your feet on the ground.

If you would like to sit on the floor, you might want to use a meditation stool to kneel on, or a meditation cushion, or yoga block(s) if you want to sit cross-legged. A rolled-up towel or blanket placed just behind the sitting bones can be helpful too. You're looking to assume a position that allows your knees to rest on the ground. Raising the hips and/or tilting the pelvis with the aid of these props is helpful for most people. Generally, your hips should be higher than your knees as this has an impact on comfort and also breathing physiologically (unless posing for some awful stock photo for Google, in which case assume a fake smile and an uncomfortable unsustainable arm position!).

Jokes aside, sustainability for the duration of the sit and for long-term health is the key. If you have some stiffness when you end a sit, that's fine, as long as you've not cut off blood supply to an area to the extent that it's gone "dead". A good rule of thumb is that if normal feeling and function returns within a minute or so of "stretching out", then the position was fine. If you still can't walk 20 minutes after a session ends . . . get some further help with your posture! Common sense really.

Martial arts, dance and yoga classes may help you meditate more comfortably for longer periods of time. Flexible hips make having them higher than the knees easier, and movement generally helps with overall bodily ease. Chronic tension and structural issues may cause pain during meditation. Ironically a lack of movement in life, as is so common today, will make sitting still hard, but old injuries, etc. can also cause issues. Work with, and around, how you are. In our experience with thousands of people worldwide, there is ALWAYS a way, no matter what your body is like – though sometimes experimentation and perseverance are needed.

Standing

Standing meditation is associated with strength and wakefulness, and is practised in some Buddhist, Taoist, and martial arts traditions. Many meditators use it when they're sleepy in order to stay awake, or when "floating off" as the extra sensations in the legs that it promotes gives one more "ground". Given that many people nowadays spend a lot of time sitting, and this can disconnect the legs, standing may rebuild this link, and help us "come back down to earth".

Standing is equally useful if you want to develop a sense of power or confidence in your body. It's a nice thing to practise as a "lite" practice too, whilst you are queuing or waiting somewhere – assisting in transfer to daily life once you've done some more formal standing meditation.

TIPS FOR STANDING MEDITATION

Stand as still as is comfortable with the knees not totally locked and the feet 15-30 cm apart. You will not be completely motionless and are likely to become aware of subtle micro adjustments for stability. Incorporate this into your meditation.

It can be surprisingly challenging to stand still for a long time and be comfortable. Practices like yoga, tai chi and qigong can help you develop your standing meditation practice. You could start with standing for short periods of time, alternating with sitting or walking.

If you have low blood pressure you may feel dizzy and need to move from time to time. If you feel dizzy, take a few steps or bend forwards to take your head below your heart for a few breaths.

Lying down

Lying-down meditation is not often recommended due to it increasing the likelihood of falling asleep. However, some schools of meditation recommend it because it can be the most comfortable and therefore least distracting position for many people. For those who are agitated, anxious or angry, and have minimal chance of falling asleep, it may be ideal to help them relax enough to focus. The extra relaxation of the body from postural muscles not being used may also be helpful for embodiment.

Out of the four primary postures, lying-down is most associated with relaxation and healing. It can be useful if you want to meditate and allow your body to rest at the same time. It's also a position often used in the type of death meditation where you imagine being dead. More about death meditations in a later chapter (please note death meditation is not recommended if you are experiencing depression, anxiety, suicidal thoughts, or if you are in an active grief process).

TIPS FOR LYING DOWN MEDITATION

Lying-down meditation is generally done lying on your back, with your legs straight or your knees bent. Keeping your knees bent and your feet standing on the floor about hip-width apart helps to keep a

level of alertness and may also be more comfortable for your lower back. If you find your knees wobbling around a lot you can tie a scarf, tie or belt around them for support in that position.

Alternatively, you could rest the back of your knees over a bolster or pillow. A small bend in the knees helps to relax the lower back for most.

If you find your head tipping back uncomfortably far, with your chin sticking up in the air, then use a thin yoga block, a narrow book or a small cushion under your head.

To stop you from falling asleep, you could keep your forearms and hands off the floor. Keep your elbows resting on the floor with the forearms and hands held directly above your elbows. If you get sleepy, your hands will wobble or drop to the floor and wake you up.

Keeping both feet and head cool may also help you stay awake, as can not lying on a bed or other very comfortable surface. If not too brutal a wooden floor may be excellent, and a thin yoga mat better than a thick fluffy carpet. We also like doing this outside on grass where breeze and gentle background noise assist with wakefulness.

Walking

Walking meditation is practised formally in different schools, such as the Zen and Theravada traditions. When practised formally, it might involve something like walking up and down a gravel path very slowly, whilst focusing on your breath or the sensations of your feet on the ground. Breath and steps can be linked, or not, and there are some fast-walking forms used to promote wakefulness between sitting sessions. There is no one way, except it's always done with awareness.

There is also a practice of "aimless wandering". The idea is to walk for the sake of walking, without any particular destination. To "just walk". This is very good for those of us who find it hard to let go and get out of "doing mode."

It can even be practised informally – for example when you walk to the shop. It's particularly useful for transfer to life – we walk around all the time, even if only from the house to the car, from your desk to the kitchen, etc. Daily life offers many opportunities to practise this, again boosted by sometimes doing it more formally.

TIPS FOR WALKING MEDITATION

Walking meditation can be a good way into meditation if you find it difficult to be still. You could alternate sitting or standing with walking, which is the schedule used on many retreats. It's often a good idea to slow down so you have more of a chance to notice your body and/or your surroundings – for example, enjoying nature around you and being aware of your senses. This non-habitual slow walking also forces many to concentrate on balance, which is a useful aid. In formal practice, a repetitive route, like going up and down a path or in circles, is often used, as more varied walks may prove distracting.

Whilst walking, you can notice the sensations in your body, the way you walk, how your feet move and touch the ground. You can be aware of your breathing and your senses. There are various options but after experimenting, pick one per session.

Naturally, do not walk across roads while fully focused on the body! And if you are in a busy outdoor environment, please maintain an awareness of what is going on around you. High-traffic areas such as shopping centres or the metro can be used for a challenge with sufficient practice, but again, be careful.

Spine position and problems

In all of the upright meditation positions, the spine should be naturally upright with the curves of the spine present and with your head balanced comfortably on your spine. Generally one should avoid the military "stick up the arse" or "lazy hippie/teenager" extremes. More sophisticatedly, one could think of these as two ends of a scale – a range to explore within.

This sounds simple enough, but many of us have developed a fairly fixed posture as a result of gravity, the type of work we've done throughout our life, injuries, poorly-designed furniture and screens, and even our personality types (as any body-therapist will tell you). Muscles become shortened and lengthened, weakened and gain chronic tension and this makes comfort and flexibility difficult to achieve.

What this essentially means is that our posture is physically or neurotically stuck in one mode – e.g., slumped or extended (for "defeated" or hypervigilant trauma) – and this will have a negative impact on our meditation. Prolonged meditation is an intensely physical, near athletic achievement for many modern people.

It may take some time before you can be comfortable sitting or standing still without additional support for your back. It's part of the practice and therapeutic movement forms such as Feldenkrais and Alexander Technique, as well as yoga, tai chi and qigong, can be very helpful. Avoid becoming rigid about pushing through discomfort – if you notice tension, move a little bit. If your legs go to sleep, shift and move. If your knees hurt, move to another position. Over time your postural grace and range will improve, and the ease with which you can be in meditation postures will increase.

Adjustment Enquiries

Let's return to the metaphor for posture that relates to both spinal position and developing a more subtle attitude like a guitar string. How to make it not too loose so that it can't strike the note, but not too tight so that it snaps?

Simply asking yourself if you are too tight or too loose will often guide you towards a useful adjustment.

Looking around a retreat at others meditating is also instructive as other people's "string tightness" is more obvious than our own at times!

Other useful enquiries for posture include:

- Is this position useful?
- Is this position healthy and kind?
- Is this position sustainable?
- Is this position a performance or an identity (e.g., "the good student", "the spiritual one", "the Zen tough guy", etc)?
- What position would be optimal now?

Often we know the answer intuitively and can adjust accordingly.

More postural variations

Most schools say there is one way to sit or stand "correctly". Instead, we prefer to see posture as a tool to optimise one's practice. The "settings" that can be adjusted within the basic tools of the four positions include spinal position (as discussed), gaze and hand position.

Gaze

Many people meditate with their eyes closed. While this may significantly reduce distraction and help you focus on the body, it is more likely to make you sleepy. It also doesn't help with transferring your meditation skills into life off the cushion – after all, it would be very impractical to keep your eyes closed all the time.

We recommend alternating practicing with your eyes open and closed whilst sitting, lying or standing, as well as directing your gaze down towards the ground, directly in front of you, and also up. Opening your eyes and lifting your gaze can give you a sense of increased clarity as well as wakefulness. At other times it may be useful to close your eyes to reduce distraction. Experiment as ever.

You can also change the quality of your focus, for instance softening your gaze to increase the level of your peripheral vision, or focusing intently on something. Again, both will have a different effect on how you are and how you experience yourself as a body in the world.

For beginners, it can be helpful to close your eyes during a body scan, to enable you to focus on the felt sense of your body more easily. For intermediate and advanced practitioners, practise with your eyes open (or move to this later in a sit) to see if you can still deeply and consistently sense the detail of your embodied experience.

Hand positions

In the yoga and Buddhist traditions, there are many different hand and finger positions used in meditation. You may wish to experiment with different positions to see how they change your embodiment during meditation. It's generally useful to relax your hands, on your lap or on your thighs in seated meditation, or on your belly or the floor if you are lying down. You can position your palms up or down, which can change your state (up tends to be lighter, down more "grounded"). Mudras are special hand positions which may have esoteric uses beyond the scope of this book, such as the classic Zen position of touching all fingers and both thumbs together as if holding an egg. Such positions can increase focus and regulate attitude (e.g., being too loose or too intense is quicker to feel).

Again, the effect of these different options is quite subtle and may be more useful for more experienced practitioners to play with.

Hands can also be used to touch the body to increase awareness of various areas, which we will return to later.

CHAPTER 3

EMBODIED MEDITATION TECHNIQUES

THE SIX CORE TECHNIQUES OF EMBODIED MEDITATION

While different things work for different people at different times, we have found that this set of six techniques is helpful for most people. Please try all of these several times, and if you'd like to really get the benefits from this approach, then pick one to commit to for a period (two months is good). Use one as the regular core of your meditation. There is also a section in the next chapter on choosing and establishing a practice.

Note that timings are specifically not given so they can be expanded and contracted as you like, and all can be done in the four basic postures. Experienced practitioners can of course simply use this approach as loose inspiration or blend them with techniques already well known to them.

Aims, difficulty, methods, enquiries and movement

For each method we detail why you would do it – the aim. While too much goal direction can be unhelpful for meditation, it is very helpful to know what you are trying to gain from a practice. On some deep, abstract spiritual level there's truth in "going nowhere, doing nothing", but this isn't usually helpful as an orienting principle!

The aim can also be the expected result of the meditation, though this isn't set in stone, and as previously mentioned the "how" in many ways leads this more than the "what" of the technique. Note that some meditations may develop a skill as the aim but it may not always be relaxing nor pleasant, as a beginner who mistakes meditation for stress relief might find. Though of course a degree of ease helps a lot and if meditations are overwhelming feel free to change them or shift practice. While a degree of difficulty is to be expected, too much challenge isn't helpful either.

The key "learning zone" to stay in is a moderation of challenge to engage you and indicate growth may well be happening, but not too much so it demotivates you or drains you for life. Critically if one is well-resourced in life the opportunity for growth through challenge exists, whereas if one is depleted or struggling generally in life, there is a necessity for easier, more restorative practice. Likewise, any natural enthusiasm for a technique should be followed to some degree, but also balanced with an element of discipline as to what one needs (following aims that match what one requires, as opposed to simply what one likes). For beginners, ease and pleasure are key – establishing any regular meditation practice at all is hard enough!

Hopefully we give a clear "how" for each technique – this is the method. Most meditations have a simple "do this" operational technique which we hope makes them practical and accessible. A pet dislike of ours is instructions like "empty your mind" which have no method given! "OK mate, HOWWWW do I empty my mind??!!". In addition to the primary method, we sometimes give enquiries which provide a different more exploratory way into each technique. Some students FAR prefer this approach, while others get little from it and need direct instructions, so we present both options.

One departure from many traditional practices is that in addition to the main technique, we encourage some small movements, guided breathing, postural changes, touch and even sounding (making noises). The reason for this is that all these engage the body and are excellent "anchors" to the present moment for the hyper-distracted modern mind. The idea here is not to fidget, wriggle or to entertain yourself, but more as a subtle helping hand back to presence. These can be excellent if you find yourself drifting off, or are very tired or agitated (most people are simultaneously both these days much of the time), and usually you can gradually minimise their use in a session, moving towards stillness.

I (Mark) find these excellent with my ADHD as it gives me a little more sensation and variety to "hold onto". On group retreats I often move very, very subtly so as not to distract others; and minimise sounding (e.g. sighs)! Recently I have been further inspired in this method by somatic meditation teacher Jamie McHugh[10] who has somewhat formalised this approach.

10 http://www.somaticexpression.com/

THE BASIC BODY SCAN

Goal: To develop body awareness (CCDD) and concentration.
It will also be relaxing and reduce stress in many cases.

Theory:

The body scan involves focussing our awareness on the body, throughout the body. It is perhaps THE fundamental practice in this book and in many traditions. It can be done in different ways, for example:

- Systematically – scanning from top to bottom or vice versa, or outside to inside
- Responsively – bringing awareness to what's most noticeable. Using anything that calls your attention as the anchor
- Completely – feeling the whole body at once in its entirety

Whichever scanning method you are doing, the idea is to bring awareness to the whole body over a period of time, not just the surface or a specific part of the body. Do not ignore areas that are numb, or less noticeable for other reasons such as the back – this is a risk of the (often easier) responsive method if used alone. Often we use systematic body scanning as the standard technique, and emergent for when we're more distracted and needing an easier "anchor", but there is no hard and fast rule. Whole body awareness is challenging for most (and not the same as rapid scanning). One can also play unusual games with awareness to challenge skills, for example being aware of just one side of the body at a time, or rapidly jumping between areas. Experiment and find what works for you.

People may call this technique a "basic" practice but there are people who do this as their only practice their entire life, and it is enough. Trust that more detail and profundity opens with it in time too, and look for this. An attitude of open-minded curiosity is often helpful to "go deeper".

Method:

Bring awareness to the physical sensations of the body, and when the mind drifts, bring it gently but firmly back. Be aware of yourself as a body. Inhabit yourself.

As with all concentration meditations, the method here is to keep returning the attention to the focus (the body) whenever you get distracted. Many times, if necessary! Do not worry if you do not have an empty mind. It is normal to become distracted by thoughts, especially planning; and by other senses such as outside sounds. If you notice you are distracted, great, you are present! Come back to the body with a determined, but kind, attitude (berating yourself will not help).

One can use noting and labelling sensations as an addition to aid these techniques, by opening to a moment and allowing a sensation to really "sink in", before naming it internally or out-loud. Examples include, "tightening", "expanding", "relaxing", "warmth", etc. Noting and labelling can aid concentration, as will guided meditations for most (many are online including ours at **https:// embodiedmeditationbook.com**), so use either approach if you are very distracted.

Be careful to actually feel the body, not just to imagine or visualise the body.

Enquiries:

- Where am I not feeling? Where are the blindspots? Am I subtly avoiding an area?
- How deeply am I feeling? What would it mean to be really present to the body now?

- Am I aware OF or aware AS? What would the latter mean as an experience?
- What in more detail is this feeling?
- How much can I feel at once?
- Where feels more or less like "me"?

Touch, breathwork and movement:

If any area is hard to feel, it can be helpful to add gentle movement, breathe "into" the area[11] or touch yourself slowly and gently on the surface of the area. Of course, doing this meditation after something like a shower, exercise, sauna or massage which brings awareness to the whole body through sensation can be helpful too.

---

11 Breathe so there's movement in the direction of the area and use visualisation to support this

EMOTIONAL "DIGESTION" MEDITATION

Goal: To process emotions.

To "get over" stuff. To release micro-trauma. For holistic well-being. To both learn from, and feel good again, after a difficult life event.

Theory:

This is similar to complete body awareness but it focuses on areas that have an emotive tone – often the face, throat, chest, and belly. The idea here is to sit "with" the feelings – both physical and emotional. While in English the word "feeling" covers both of these, in Buddhist practice they are referred to as the "first and second foundations of mindfulness". It is probably intuitively known by most people that sadness (2nd foundation) is not the same as indigestion (1st), for example. The latter is merely bodily sensations, while the former has an additional subtle, almost non-local, meaningful and emergent quality.

Awareness is a kind of emotionally digestive "enzyme", helping emotions transform naturally in beneficial ways. You could also think of this meditation as a form of gentle bodily self-empathy.

Any concentration meditation will stop us self-generating emotions with story (by interrupting our narrative with another focus) and so will be stress relieving if we are generating unpleasant emotions. This meditation is especially good for helping deal with this as it also works on a level of natural processing that mere distractions do not – distracting ourselves from emotions by ignoring or suppressing them doesn't encourage any processing and transforming of emotion.

Method:

Bring awareness to whole body emotional sensations, and when the mind drifts, bring it gently back. Stay with them non-reactively.

Stay present to physical and emotional sensations, allowing them to change and transform (without trying to force this). The stance of sitting with a grieving friend is very helpful for this technique. The idea is to stay kindly present and not interfere. Be with your "heart" (your overall bodily emotional tone), and other specific sensations that feel significant or emotive, in the here and now.

You may notice sighs, relaxations of chronic tension, temperature changes or other indications of release. With time a clear, often pleasant, felt sense of having processed or "digested" emotions is noticeable. For many this can take as little as a few minutes, but there are also "layers" of this in most people. For bigger more impactful emotional states such as acute grief and historical trauma it can take days or even years[12].

Importantly, while thoughts, memories, images, etc. may well come up, DO NOT follow these or start analysing yourself. This is not body-assisted therapy (which does have value but is different). This is just sitting with oneself gently, allowing witnessing with self-empathy to bring naturally flowing change. If you follow a train of thought it will reset the "digestion" process. Similarly, you may have creative urges or want to contact someone to tell them something – do not follow these during the meditation[13].

12 In these cases, there can be tears of release or unusual sensations like a knot being released deep inside one's guts, or like a warm egg being cracked open inside you.
13 Embodied meditation will almost certainly make you more creative by the way, but this is not the intention, more a by-product. If you want this as a goal, for example if you are an artist or poet, then split your practice into two clear sets with different intentions.

Enquiries:

- Where do I feel this emotion in my body?
- What does it feel like? What are the qualities of the sensations in my body associated with this emotion?
- What part of my emotional experience am I pushing away?
- What feels most meaningful in my body now?
- How do I feel about how I am feeling right now? I.e., is there a noticeable tendency to want to suppress/escape emotion, or make it go away?
- Is there physical tension around the emotion I can let go of? Can I surrender to the feeling more (without being overwhelmed)?

Touch, breathwork and movement:

- Placing a hand on the heart and/or the belly/womb can be very soothing
- Gentle movement to encourage relaxation of tension accompanying emotions may be helpful. Emotions are movements so let them move, though this can be done with subtle movements
- Sounding (e.g., conscious sighs) can be used to let go of emotion, and there's a huge range of breathwork possible to aid digestion, such as briefly holding and then releasing the breath with emotion, NOT using the breath to soothe, and other techniques which are beyond the scope of this book. Many of these will come naturally though, as they are intuitive body wisdom we have to actively repress, more than skills we learn

EMBODIED BREATH AWARENESS

Goal: To develop breath awareness and concentration
For many this will also be relaxing and pleasant.

Theory:

Mindfulness of the breath in the body is part of most approaches to meditation. To ensure you are doing it in an embodied way, make sure you practise an extensive, all-encompassing awareness of where you can feel your breath in your body, as opposed to just one point in the body. This could mean feeling the whole body moving with the breath, or just having a background sense of the body while being mostly focused on one point.

Practising awareness of the breath only in one place in your body, like at the tip of your nose as is commonly done, can lead to disassociation from other parts of your body and emotional "bypassing". Although it is a valid form of concentration practice, this method could exacerbate the incompleteness of being that embodied meditation aims to remedy. It's not bad, but is not helpful for the aim here.

Breath awareness is a very classic meditation technique for several good reasons. Three of these are:

1. The breath is a very, very sensitive indicator of our body-mind states.
2. It is constantly changing so it provides novel stimuli.
3. Working with it can translate easily into daily life (as we are always breathing).

Breath is deeply associated with life itself. The removal of this element causes death quicker than any other (as compared with say sleep or food). There is also a cross-cultural association through language (e.g., "spirit") and mythology (e.g., God breathing life into dirt to create people).

Method:

Bring awareness to the physical sensations of breathing. When the mind drifts, bring it gently back.

While there are options and variations here, we usually encourage people to focus their attention deep within the lower abdomen, and the movement of the breath beyond this, potentially into the whole body. While very subtle, it may even be possible to feel movement in your toes, head and finger caused by the breath! Stay present with the gentle pulsating jellyfish-like expansion and relaxation of the whole body as you breathe.

The chest can also be used, for instance if the lower abdomen has a traumatic association, though we have found this can be anxiety-provoking for some, and less grounded. Most people today need to "get down" into the body so the belly is our default. For complete beginners we ask them where it is easiest to feel the breath (e.g. the nose) and start there.

Usually breath meditation is done with the mouth closed to avoid a dry mouth, though if this is impossible it's OK[14].

Counting the breath can be a good tool to aid concentration. Do make sure you're focusing mostly on the sensations of breath rather than the counting though . . . because you know, embodiment :-) Perhaps let the counting go after a few minutes to simply feel and follow your breath.

It is important not to deliberately change the breath . . . which is actually quite difficult but valuable as a practice in and of itself, developing the skills of patience and non-interference. However, the

---

14 You may find your saliva increases and you need to swallow as you relax out of a mild "fight-flight" mode into a literal "rest and digest" mode every time you meditate. You will also likely get shinier eyes as you blink rate is decreased though relaxation (again, a stress level thing) and your eyes become more moist. On retreats this is very noticeable in most people by day 3-4, as is everyone becoming more beautiful both because of your perception shifting and their chronic stress dropping away! We call this the "retreat spa" . . . which can be one compounding factor in the silent "retreat romance" where you may have a crush on another retreatant - for several psychological reasons including projection of good feelings. Don't worry, they usually go away.

breath will transform with awareness: slowing down in most cases, and with the pauses in between breaths opening up. Awareness of these pauses can be especially fruitful in our experience.

Enquiries:

Enquiries are also possible as a method, but again, keep them felt not theoretical:

- How do I know I'm breathing now?
- Where can I feel the breath most clearly in my body?
- Where else can I feel the breath in my body?
- What is the very edge of where I can feel the breath? Is there anywhere in my body I cannot feel my breath? Where's the limit?
- What is the quality of the breath?
- How is it to track the rhythm of the breath? The beginning, middle and end. The "seasons" or "cycles" of the breath, if you will.
- How can I connect to the life-delivering qualities of the breath? How is breath life?
- How is it to breathe in harmony with the photosynthesising plants of the planet (hey breathe out and you breathe in, and vice versa)? A visualisation can help for this one.

The breath is hugely profound in some very non-obvious ways. We encourage you deeper into the mystery and adventure of it!

Touch, breathwork and movement:

- It may be helpful to place your hand(s) on different parts of the body where you can feel your breath – again, the abdomen is a good place, and/or the chest. Or use touch to help "open up" areas to the breath.
- Allow your meditation posture to slightly move/adapt to the in-breath and out-breath. For example, noticing how a particular

part of the breathing cycle may feel like an invitation to relax or sit up a bit straighter. This can become a subtle wave or pulse.

- While this practice is about NOT changing the breath, paradoxically using subtle holds and elongations can aid this. Experiment.

PLEASURE MEDITATION

Goal:

To develop body awareness, concentration and awareness of "like-dislike" in the body. To motivate meditation practice[15]. Also to increase awareness of enjoyment, to develop a more enjoyable relationship to the body, and enjoy life more beyond this![16]

Theory:

To become aware of whether you like, dislike or feel neutral about sensations in the body is extremely helpful on various fronts. This is what pushes us around after all, motivating everything from noble actions to severe damaging addictions. One way to get better at spotting such forces is to focus on what is pleasant, which as well as developing the skill of identifying pleasure, will also make you want to meditate more. We have a perceptual negativity bias, so it's not like you'll stop noticing pain and discomfort, but you may become more intimate in your day-to-day life with what pleasure feels like in your body and learn to enjoy your body more as a result.[17]

For those of us prone to the extremes of either addictions and hedonism, or living in a "dry" or Victorian way, this meditation may be especially useful. There's also a cultural piece here and we sometimes joke that this is the Italian or Brazilian meditation[18]. This meditation

---

15 This technique is essentially Pavlovian as the very nature of it rewards and reinforces our desire to meditate. You could think of it as "somatic doggy biscuit/treat" meditation :-)

16 Credit to Shinzen Young for introducing Mark to this one.

17 I (Karin) remember one mindful moment where I realised I was feeling pleasant but couldn't quite figure out what the nature of the pleasure was. I tuned into my body and realised it was contentment. This was the first time I noticed what contentment feels like "as a body". This was years after being told that as a yogi I "should" be cultivating contentment but wasn't really told how. Since then I recognise it more often and more easily, which seems to grow my level of contentment with life.

18 For an especially grueling place to practise this one we recommend the Moulin de Chaves in France, which last time we checked had three types of French cheese to eat and a river to swim in, though we know some other rough places in Scotland, Greece and Tuscany too.

can also be excellent to help with food and sex issues, both in terms of excess or "anorexic" tendencies.

Method:

Bring awareness to the physical sensations of pleasure in the body. When the mind drifts, bring it gently back. Enjoy the pleasure without attachment (contraction) or fantasy.

Follow enjoyment – look for areas that feel pleasurable or at least OK. The out-breath, not standing, belly and jaw release are all pleasurable for most – at least subtly. See how deeply you can enjoy the enjoyment. Let it "soak in".

Enquiries:

As ever, keep enquiries embodied and avoid theoretical thought fancies.

- How do you know pleasure is enjoyable? What is pleasure?
- How does pleasure spread or move?
- How does it impact breathing and muscle tone generally?
- What stops pleasure being enjoyable? Notice any "grasping" tension if you're wanting to keep the pleasure, or fear that it will leave.
- Is any part of you holding back from enjoying the pleasure? Is there associated guilt or a limit to what is allowable? Is there anything bad in the pleasure?
- How is pleasure the friend of embodiment?

Touch, breathwork and movement:

- Can you create a pleasurable sense in the body with touch or gentle movement?

- If there is grasping or fear? Can you identify where this is felt in the body? If there is contraction, are you able to release it?
- Sigh, groan, moan, "yuuummm", make your neighbours jealous, or concerned! For most North Europeans and Americans, loosening up around pleasure sounds and breath is liberating.

EMBODIED KINDNESS MEDITATION (AKA: METTA)

Goal:

To become kinder. Also to be less afraid, angry, reactive, impatient, (anything against how things are), etc. It's also a concentration practice to keep our focus on kindness, and a body awareness practice.

Theory:

The cultivation of "universal friendliness" through meditation is a part of many kinds of Buddhism, and there are of course equivalent practices in other traditions. It was, however, deeply radical when first practised and remains that way in its breadth. It isn't only "love thy neighbour as oneself" – already a huge step – it's love everyone, the animals, the plants, the black death. Love reality itself. This is "friendliness" in the widest possible sense, or if you prefer "well-wishing safety" – not wanting harm to come to anyone or anything. This of course includes oneself. It is not equivalent to tolerating bullshit and bad behaviour in the name of love, agreeing with everyone, nor having to hang out with everyone.

Another way to think about metta, is as an aspect of what is now translated a little dryly as "mindfulness". While concentration practices and "heart'" practices, such as metta, are sometimes thought of as separate, this is not the case. Such techniques require concentration (so double up for developing this). In fact, truly accepting the present moment, no matter how it presents itself, is an act of kindness. They are two sides of the same coin really.

There are several main methods used in classical versions of this technique such as internal repetition of phrases and visualisation. In our approach, these can be used, but we stress the direct bodily development. Intentionality is still key.[19]

---

19 Credit to Rob Burbea for introducing me (Mark) to how embodied metta could be, and trauma/aikido teacher Paul Linden for some of the aspects of metta presented here.

Method:

Start with a brief body scan, emphasising acceptance of what is in a kind manner. This is a good base for what comes next and could actually be the complete practice.

Now choose a goodwill phrase such as "may I be happy, may I be well, may I be at ease, may I be safe, may I be free, etc". Say it to yourself internally in your first language. Nothing too specific, but something that leads to happiness and genuine deep wellbeing for everyone (as later you are invited to use the same phrase for all others). Not "may I eat all the cake and make loads of cash", nor "may my headache go away". Repeat each phrase internally slowly, while feeling the impact on the body and allowing the words to "land' after each phrase. Encourage your body to soften and open, to relax and expand symmetrically. Both relaxation and expansion matter.

With practise one can alter one's bodily state directly without the phrases. Other positive states that are not exactly the same as metta can also be cultivated in a similar way.

Phrases can "kick start" the somatic process. Authenticity is a factor here, and connecting with a sincere intention for safety and wellbeing is key. Don't just say it, mean it – as best as you can. Sometimes you have to fake it till you make it though! You may need to find a way of meaning it more in the body (for example a small smile may be useful). You can add a visualisation like radiant light of a colour you associate with kindness coming from the centre of your chest. Keep feeling and utilising the body to learn to embody kindness. Learn to do what happens naturally at certain times, more consciously, so you can do it more of the time. Simple really.

The next step is to move on to someone you find easy to feel kindness for (but don't have sexual attraction to). Use the phrases ("may you . . .") and the bodily aspects again. If visualising, you could imagine light going from you to them.

If you suffer from self-hatred or low self-esteem you may want to do this stage first. Experiment.

You can then move on to a neutral person (maybe someone you see daily but don't know well, like the bus driver on your regular route, or someone you just met). Then a harder person (but go easy here if it is someone you have trauma around). Lastly, include everyone/all beings. If you get stuck or it feels forced, go back to yourself or the easy person. Keep with the body, this isn't some nice daydream!

If you get "stuck" and it starts to feel inauthentic, or you are just under-resourced, you can always return (and even stay with) yourself or the easy person.

You can also work geographically in visualised expanding circles, or through categories like animals/plants/people, occupations, nationalities, etc. Such things can keep it fresh, allowing you to be creative, but make sure to **stay with the body!**[20]

Enquiries:

- What is the shape of love? How does it feel in the body?
- How can I do love as an action?
- How am I when genuinely friendly?
- What in my body is not loving (replace this with relaxed expansion if you can)?
- In what subtle ways am I pushing reality away right now?
- If I was truly not hostile what would change now?

Touch, breathwork and movement:

- Putting your hand(s) on the heart may be useful, as can stroking the chest on upper arms, or even giving yourself a hug (google "self care pose embodied yoga principles" for more).

---

20 See also Martin Aylward's book "Awake Where You Are" which has a detailed part on metta and related meditations, and "metta legends" Tara Brach and Sharon Salzberg.

- Usually softening the "edges" of the breath allowing it to be more circular helps, as does a very, very gentle active encouragement of the in-breath and totally passive letting go of the out-breath.
- Extending the hands forwards on sending kindness, and bringing them back towards you to receive it, can also enhance the practice.

WELCOME MEDITATION

Goal:

To develop a greater acceptance of the body and sensation. Also a concentration practice. To lead to more equanimity in life.

Theory:

If you are not-fully enlightened, on some level you will be fighting reality and the life of your own body. Sometimes this leads us to ignore sensations, sometimes to push them away, sometimes to distract ourselves, etc. This can lead to many harmful things such as emotional denial, being cut off from ourselves, and addictive tendencies to not feel. While these are understandable survival strategies we develop as children, and judging them is not helpful, it is often useful to practise something else.

Welcome meditation sounds simple, but is a profoundly difficult meditation for many people (if you are really paying attention to how you do not fully embrace everything) and more profound than it may initially seem.

All embodied meditation is about "being with what is", yet this welcome meditation explicitly focuses on this. We also call it "yes" or "full yes" meditation. You may have noticed that while we present six core techniques, in many ways they are different facets of the same thing.

Method:

Feel your body as per the body scan, or any way you like. Say "yes" or "welcome" to yourself, and note any sensations that arise within the body. Do this as an internal "mantra" in your first language. Note the sensation of acceptance – often a release of tension – and consciously replicate this. Examine how you do them so you can deliberately practise them; this is the core technique of embodied change.

If you find yourself resisting, denying or "pushing away" sensation or emotion of any kind, see if you can tolerate opening up and saying yes to it instead for just a little while longer. If you need to "look away" that's fine. The practice is simply staying with it a bit longer than you might otherwise in order to grow this capacity. The idea is not to brutally confront everything at once at any cost! "A bit more" adds up and you will grow.

Open, relax, feel. Open some more.

Enquiries:

- What is the body of really saying a "full yes"?
- Is your "yes" complete?
- What is it to truly welcome (as opposed to say merely tolerate)? How can you do this in the body?
- Are you fully enthusiastically receptive?
- How does any resistance you might notice feel in the body?
- What do you do in the body when resistance ceases? Can you do this on purpose?

Touch, breathwork and movement:

- Hand(s) resting palms up or out may be useful, and eyes open often helps.
- A letting go soft outbreath, and a subtly actively drawing in in-breath (like smelling perfume or a loved one) can be useful.
- Movements that help you to relax, open and soften will support this.

SIX MORE EMBODIED MEDITATIONS

These tend not to be people's daily "bread and butter" meditations; however, they are all worth practising a few times for deeper, or particular insights.

4 ELEMENTS MEDITATION

Goal:

To develop greater awareness of the different aspects of the body and how they affect our embodiment, both on and off the cushion.

Theory:

The body has different qualities that can be explored separately to learn more about them. The four elements model (earth, water, fire and air) is a very old model, and provides a way to think about our constituents, how our moods change, and how people differ. There are for example five and six elements models and even more modern psychometric systems. Four elements is however primal, intuitive and will give almost anyone a better sense of their own and other's embodiment.

Also, to be clear, we know there are not literally four types of particles in the body, though they do equate to the three states of matter and heat/movement energy in physics.

Method:

Bring awareness to the four elements in the body.

A good starting point for becoming aware of the elements in the body is to approach awareness of them a bit like a body scan. As you practise, go through the four elements and notice whether, where and how you can sense them in your body.

You can use body parts:

Earth – lower body below waist
Water – The hips and belly
Fire – The chest
Air – The throat up

Or work with states of matter within the body:

Earth – solids parts of you like the bones, nails and teeth
Water – bodily liquids like blood, urine, saliva, and tears
Fire – the warmth and movement of the body
Air – the gases within us such as breath, air-filled cavities and
    even space within molecules (sometimes the fifth element)

Also with HOW you scan:

Earth – Slowly and systematically
Water – Fluidly, relationally and receptively
Fire – Fiercely, passionately and with purpose
Air – In a fun, free, non-attached way

As a more advanced approach you can also work with the four elements in meditation in a more subtle way. In embodied practice, we often refer to the four elements earth, water, fire and air to indicate four different aspects of being. Most people can easily relate to this. For example, if you know me (Mark), you might know I'm quite a fiery guy and you can probably guess what that means. Indications of fieriness are that I speak fast, am passionate about embodiment, and I wrote this book in a month . . . And if you know me (Karin), you might know I am much more earthy than Mark, which means I speak and move more slowly, I'm very organised and I am better at spell-checking than him.

We all embody all four elements to a lesser or greater degree in different contexts in our lives and each has potential benefits and downsides. You can read more about this in my (Mark's) earlier books. Becoming aware of how you embody the qualities of the four elements in meditation can be very useful. For example, focusing on the earth element underneath us (as in sitting, standing, lying or walking on the planet) can help us to settle into calmness more easily. Focusing on the water element might help us to not tighten up too much in our practice – remember the example of not being too tight or loose in our approach? Focusing on fire can help us to stay awake and being aware of air can help us not to take it all too seriously.

Formal meditation often emphasises embodying the earth element as it is largely about slowing down or being still. The other elements can, however, be subtly emphasised in our posture and awareness.

One way of doing this is by making subtle adjustments to the meditation posture, for example taking the gaze down (emphasises earth), softening the gaze to peripheral vision or moving the gaze around (water), looking intently at something with a high degree of concentration (fire), looking up at the sky (air).

Another way is through minute postural changes. Resting the hands with the palms down and relaxing the body weight towards the ground increases earthiness, palms up or resting lightly emphasizes air. Sitting more intently upright can bring out subtle fieriness, while allowing micro adjustments in the posture allows wateriness.

Enquiries:

- What is the body of each element?
- Can you identify a felt sense of each element in the body? How does it feel?
- Which is easier and more familiar to you? Which takes more effort?
- How has any meditation tradition you have been trained in biased your elemental style?
- How has your cultural background biased your elemental style?

Touch, breath and movement:

- Explore subtle postural changes. As above: sitting more intently upright can bring out subtle fieriness, allowing micro adjustments in the posture wateriness, resting the hands with the palms down and relaxing the body weight towards the ground increases earthiness, palms up or resting lightly emphasizes air.
- Each element has a breath: fire is more pushing and in the mid-chest, water more flowing and in the upper belly, air more light and in the upper chest, earth more rhythmic and steady, and in the lowest belly.

CYCLES MEDITATION
(AWARENESS ON THE BREATH,
NOTING PARTS)

Goal:

To develop a greater awareness of the cycle of breathing, and the way nature flows.

Theory:

Another model we use a lot in embodied work is the idea of cycles. In meditation this can be used as a focus on the recurring cycle of the breath. The start of the in-breath, the middle of the in-breath, the end of the in-breath, the pause before the out-breath starts, etcetera. This can be a rich enquiry into the cyclical nature of breathing.

Method:

Be aware of your breathing and the different parts of each breath as you follow it with awareness. Notice the qualities of the ebb and flow of the breath, where you tend to rush and linger, and the overall nature of this rhythm.

Enquiries:

- How does each part of the breathing cycle feel in the body? What's its quality (for example, the out breath might feel more like "letting go")?
- Can I allow the cycle of the breath to take place without interfering?
- How do the transitions between different parts of the breath feel?

Touch, breath and movement:

- Explore how movement and stillness might emphasise / enhance each part of the breath.
- Use the speed of the breath to subtly change each "season".
- Create simple movements with your body, for example moving your hands up and down, that follow the cycles of your breath.

4 LAYERS MEDITATION - SKIN, MUSCLES/ FASCIA, BONES, MARROW

Goal:

To become more fully embodied, being aware of different body systems.

Theory:

When I (Mark) started studying experiential anatomy, through such systems as Bonnie Bainbridge Cohen's BodyMind Centering, I came to realise that the years of sitting meditation I had done "feeling the body", only accessed a very shallow part of myself and not all body systems. I had mostly only been noticing my skin and, much later, some deeper organ sensations. It is however possible to feel into layers of muscle and fascia (connective tissue in the body), the bones and even into the marrow itself.

This little meditation does not replace full experiential anatomy training but will give a taste.

Method:

Spend a little time studying some anatomy photos of parts of the body and feel your own body as you do so. Movement can also be helpful to explore.

Then meditate on whatever you were studying for some time, feeling as deeply as you can, not just imagining it (although picturing the images you saw before can help).

One can also move between the four layers: skin, muscles/fascia, bones, and marrow. Go deeper into the body and feel the different quality of each.

There are other systems too that you could explore. One could add awareness of specific organs to this. If you get stuck and cannot feel a layer, visualise it until you can. You may notice a very different "flavour" when focusing on each layer, pay attention to this.

Enquiries:

- How is it to really inhabit each layer?
- What's the felt sense of a specific layer of the body? What is its quality like to you? Heavy, light, dense, loose, etc.
- Do you habitually "live' in one layer?

Touch, breath and movement:

- How is it to move "from the bones", skin, muscles, etc.?
- Imagine breathing using each layer in the lungs, and breathing "into" each layer through the whole body. What changes?
- Explore the qualities of skin, bone, fascia, and where possible different organs, through movement and touch

BODY PARTS EXPLORED

Body parts are not all the same, they have themes and qualities. The elbow does not feel like the inner thigh, for example! To feel the hands has a profoundly different effect on the bodymind than to feel the feet. Bringing awareness to the face tends to open up different themes than bringing it to the back. And so on. For us this is both fascinating and hugely useful to explore, despite it often being ignored in traditional practice.

While this is something of an individual and cultural matter, there are some common tendencies across people that are worth looking out for. Rather than tell you all of these as we feel them, we suggest being curious as to the different qualities of parts of the body. When meditating, ask yourself what is the quality of "face" or "hand" as you feel it, or even one finger compared to the others. Get to know the "flavour" of each part of you.

One interesting side note is that all parts are artificially created by our linguistic and cultural distinctions. In some cultures, for example, the "leg" includes the foot. In others, there are separate words for the front and back of what would simply be "neck" in English.

Equally, where we "map" a body part as being/ending impacts us. Picture your arms extending down your back like wings including the latissimus dorsi muscles and the pectoral muscles in the chest, or picture the legs including the psoas muscles going right up into your core, connecting to the middle of the spine, for example, and you will likely feel and move differently.

GROUND MEDITATION

Goal:

To find a safe, relaxed ease in the body.

Theory:

While often a little loose in theory and method, the idea of "grounding" points to a very real phenomena: that people often feel disconnected from the earth, and this is anxiety provoking. The ground is a base embodied metaphor for stability and safety[21] and establishing our connection to it is deeply nourishing for most.

Method:

Settle into a meditation posture and notice where you touch the ground. Note that some find sitting, standing or lying down much easier for this meditation. Each has advantages so please experiment with different postures.

Bring your attention to the areas of your body that are connected with the ground. If your mind drifts, gently bring it back.

Let your weight settle as much as you can, drop any tension and further "land" on the ground. Relax physically as much as you can. You may want to tense and release to do this. Being aware of your sitting bones, and perhaps your perineum (the area between the genitals and the anus), touching the ground through your clothes can be very helpful[22].

---

21 Which is why earthquakes are especially freaky, let me tell you! – Mark.
22 To "find" the former sit on a hard surface like a wooden chair or a wall, to find the latter stop your pee next time you are going and locate the muscles that do this.

Notice and, if possible, enjoy any sense of happiness, emotional relaxation or safety that comes from contacting the ground and relaxing down. You may also perceive a subtle "rebound" up from it.

Breathing lower "into" the body (so that the belly moves) can also be helpful, but don't force it. Supportive visualisations can also be an aid, for example tree roots, or imaging down into the ground beneath you. Practise staying connected to the body and emotional sensations whilst using your imagination.

Enquiries:

- What is the relationship between different parts of the body and the ground? Are some parts of the body closer to / heavier / more relaxed in relation to the ground? Does this relationship change as you practise?
- How does my posture change when I am aware of the ground?
- How does my state change when I am aware of the ground?

Touch, breath and movement:

- How is it to touch the floor as I practise? For example, placing the palms down on the ground
- You can experiment with breathing deeply into the body including the pelvic floor
- Walking meditation with attentiveness on the connection, disconnection, reconnection of the feet to the ground

BREATH / PULSE MEDITATIONS

Goal:

To develop more subtle awareness of body sensation.

Also good for stress management and to aid concentration.

Theory:

One of the best ways to increase body awareness is to focus on something with more and more subtlety. Doing this with your pulse is excellent as it is throughout the whole body, and can help us get deeper into the body as well as more sensitive to sensation.

Method:

Feel your pulse where it is obvious – e.g., in the chest – and then to try and feel it where it is less obvious – perhaps the face and hands – to where it is very subtle indeed – the elbows, say. This will increase your sensitivity to it, and to the body in general[23].

Similarly, one can also increase sensitivity by following the breath to where it is far less obviously moving in the body. Naturally such "disappearance" meditations (the fading chime of a bell is more traditional) refine one's awareness, focus, and concentration.

Connecting to the heartbeat and the breath can also tune you into the nature of your embodied life itself – ever moving, delicate, strong, transient, uncertain (it could literally stop right now), etc. In terms of traditional meditation, "insight" themes of such things as the impermanence of the pulse and breathing are excellent visceral contemplations.

23 Credit to the Russian martial art of Systema, and our friend Matt Hill for this one.

Enquiries:

- Where can I feel the pulse in the body? Where can I not feel it?
- Where <u>exactly</u> does the sensation disappear?
- How would it be if this was my first / last breath / heartbeat?

Touch, breath and movement:

- Placing the hands on different parts of the body can be an aid
- The "quieting" necessary for more subtle feeling will normally encourage you to smoothen the breath
- Trying to do this meditation with any movement or sound will normally make it more challenging should you want that

MISCELLANEOUS EXTRA MEDITATIONS

Most of these meditations should be done infrequently, some perhaps just once for insight (this is not a hard rule).

CENTRES MEDITATION

Goal:

To develop more awareness of different centres of the body

Theory:

There are various systems that focus on different "centres" of the body. For some these have esoteric meanings relating to an "energy body" or belief system around "subtle energy", and if this works for you, great. They can also simply be viewed as orientating points which have particular effects when focused on and so are ways to both access parts of ourselves and change state.

It is intuitive (though partly cultural) to think of different points of the body as having meaning and "opening up" different aspects of oneself. This can also be explored experientially. While there are complex "chakra" systems, a simple three-centre meditation is a good place to start[24].

Often the belly is more bodily, solid, safe and powerful; the centre of the chest more emotional, "heartfelt", relational and connecting; and the head more intellectual, abstract and analytical. Note that while some traditions are quite "anti-head", for others it is a deeply spiritual centre, so be open to this experiential possibility.

Method:

Bring your attention to the lower belly, a few inches below the navel, and in the centre of your body, just in front of the spine. If your mind

24 Both Wendy Palmer and Judith Blackstone have influenced us here. Look up Christopher Wallis and Anodea Judith for more on chakra meditations if so inclined.

drifts, bring it gently back as per all concentration meditations. After some time, notice how this centre has impacted you – your emotions, thinking, perception, etc., and the overall quality of your being.

Do this next for the centre of the chest (again, not the surface) and then the centre of your head, noticing what changes as you shift attention.

Once you have invested some time in this practice, it becomes an excellent tool in daily life. Each centre is essentially a different "mode" you can then readily shift between. You may also notice that you have a default mode!

Enquiries:

- Does how I am change when I focus on each of these three centres? How do I change? What might be the usefulness of this?
- What is the emerging quality or wisdom of each of these parts of the body?
- Do I have a habitual centre?

Touch, breath and movement:

- Placing your hand(s) on or in front of one of the centres can be helpful
- Moving from a centre can help you access it – literally moving this part of the body first when walking for example, or moving the joints around a centre – say, rolling the pelvis to access the centre there
- Breathing "into" centres is useful. With the head this is, of course, mostly in the imagination

EMBODIED VISUALISATION

Goal:

To develop the ability to enhance meditation and access states with visualisation.

Theory:

You can use visualisation while feeling the body (embodied as opposed to simply mental visualisation) to enhance any meditation. For this you need a practised range of options that work for you personally.

Method:

Experiment with imaging different colours (a bright daffodil yellow for example will wake most people up, while a deep earth brown can be settling), natural images (mountains, rivers, fire, clouds, etc.), animals, and anything else you fancy. Have wings, grow roots, stream rainbow light, whatever, go for it!

You can also play with an imagined place, being in a particular location (e.g., a cave, forest, or cathedral), imagining yourself being there and noticing how that changes your embodiment (see the next meditation).

Different things work for different people, and there's some cultural aspect to this.

Be very careful not to completely lose track of the body with this one. With practise a kind of dialogue can develop where the body changes as a result of the visualisation but also informs the visualisation.

Enquiries:

- Does how I am change when I imagine these different things? How does it change me? I.e. Does visualising a yellow flower wake me up?
- What informs my visualisation?
- How is it to visualise only mentally vs with the body?

Touch, breath and movement:

- When you imagine a landscape or place, or an animal etc., imagine what it would be like to touch it, to feel the grass under your feet, touch the fur of the animal you're imagining, etc.
- Breathe or move subtly as the thing, e.g. use flowing movements to "become" the river, or breathe out like a dragon. Now we know this could sound a bit like a kid's drama class but trust us, done sincerely it works for many!

CULTURAL/PLACE BODY MEDITATIONS

Goal:

To discover our own conditioning by place and culture

Theory:

We embody both our own personal history and our cultural history. We are influenced by our current physical environment and our current cultural one.

Method:

It can be very useful to sit with the enquiry, "what is it to be Dutch?" (or whatever). If you have a mixed background, you can try this with

CONTEXTS OF EMBODIMENT

FOUNDATIONS
OF EMBODIMENT
CERTIFICATION

EMBODIED
FACILITATOR
COURSE

several nations, or more specific subcultures (e.g., "a Londoner?"). Feel this aspect of yourself.

Similarly, when meditating in different rooms, or more varied locations from time to time, e.g. when on holiday, notice how this impacts you. The embodiment principle of "exaggeration and contrast[25]" may be helpful for these explorations.

Enquiries:

- How is it to be . . . (fill in the blank)?
- How would I be more/less . . .?
- How does this place shape me?
- What is new or challenging for me to be here?

Touch, breath and movement:

- Walking/moving in the cultural embodiment you're exploring, or being consciously informed by the place can be helpful
- Try literally holding your culture in place
- What touch and movement is encouraged culturally or by a place? For example, do you want to thump your chest or stroke your face?
- How do your people breathe? How should you breathe here?

25 Credit: Wendy Palmer.

DEATH MEDITATION

Goal:

The purpose of reflecting on death in this context is to:

- Appreciate the embodied life we have and the fragile tenderness of that
- To be aware of the precious opportunity we have to live life fully and to make a difference in the world
- To help us realise what is really meaningful and important in our lives

Theory:

Death meditations are practised in various traditions and cultures to sharpen values, increase gratitude, and paradoxically; bring us closer to life. They may sound morbid and be difficult at first, but have great value in our experience.

Cautions – this meditation is not suitable:

- if you are depressed or anxious, or have suicidal thoughts
- if someone close to you died recently and you are in active mourning

If you don't feel well-resourced it may also not be the right time. Please take care. As an alternative, you can take a walk outside and be mindful of all the signs of impermanence all around you – for example plants and trees in different cycles of growth or decay, seasons (spring, summer, autumn, winter), etc.

If, during the meditation, it becomes too much for you; you can open your eyes, stop and become aware of your senses, centre yourself, gently move and take a walk.

The intention of a death meditation is to reflect on the reality that you are going to die. The life of a human being is finite. It is the one certainty in this life, yet we do not spend much time reflecting on it. The usefulness of reflecting on death is that it can connect us strongly to purpose, to why we are here and what is important to us in the time that we have. It can also support a deep appreciation of life whilst we have it.

Method:

Bringing attention to the impermanence of the body, your life, and everything around you.

To meditate on death, settle into stillness, with your eyes closed. You may wish to lie down to simulate being dead. Notice the darkness behind your eyelids and feel the aliveness in your body right now. Then reflect on the different ways you could die during the course of your day. You might have a stroke or a heart attack, without any warning. You might slip in the shower or get hit by a car. In your mind run through how a normal day is for you and how you could die. An accident, an assault, a fall.

If you are able to, stay with the feelings that may arise as you imagine how you could die today.

Then imagine how all the signs that you are alive, that you can sense in your body right now, will stop. One day your breath will stop. Your heart will stop beating. Your body will go cold and stiff. All these sensations of aliveness will cease. Your hearing will fade. Your sight will grow dim. You won't be able to feel, smell, touch anything.

Imagine that you'll die and that your body will disintegrate. This embodied form of you will no longer exist. If it is OK for you to do so, imagine your dead body; in the mortuary, or in a coffin, to be buried, to be burnt, to be returned to nature.

You can add imagining that all your belongings are given away and that everyone you know is also gone.

What comes up?

To finish, bring awareness to being alive again, aware as an alive human body. Take a moment to reflect on the freedom you have to do what you want with your life and all the opportunities available to you. It can be a good idea to move rigorously to re-establish your aliveness!

You may wish to write some things down to process the death meditation. For example, journal on questions like these:

- What are you going to do with the rest of your precious life?
- What are you grateful for?[26]
- What do you want to have done by the time you die?
- What is important to you?
- What are you here to do?
- Who are you here to love/be with?
- What or who do you want to be in service to?

---

26 Embodied gratitude meditation with a physical gesture like a bow can be a great meditation in and of itself to enhance happiness

EDGE OF THE BODY: YOU-NOT YOU

Goal:

To explore the non-separate nature of the body and open, expansive meditative states.

Theory:

Where do you end?

The enquiry at the heart of this meditation is where you label each sensation you notice as either "inside" or "outside". After some time a shift can happen where this distinction seems artificial. Noticing that the body has no clear "edge", but at least feels like it extends just beyond the skin, can also be helpful.

Method:

Sit with the enquiry, "where do I end?" Try and notice the very edge of the skin and see if you can feel just outside this. Note if the edge is not clear.

A second method[27] is to label all sensations that arise as either "inside (me)" or "outside". After a while you may become curious how you are making this distinction, or it may start to seem artificial.

Enquiries:

- Where do I begin and end? Is there a clear edge? What does it feel like?
- Where is the exact edge?

27 Credit to Shinzen Young for this.

Touch, breath and movement:

- Try placing your hands on your skin and/or just above it. Move the hands away from and back to the body, following itscontours. When do you stop feeling the connection?
- When does your breath become you? When is it in and when is it out?

BODILY SOUNDS, SIGHTS, SMELLS AND TASTES

You could guess that all "embodied" meditations use only the body as a focus, but one can also use the body's reaction and relation to any other sense. Senses are never really separate.

You could meditate on your body's response to music or mantra; bird song or the sound of breaking waves; a bell chiming or to visual art; perfume or food. Food and our relationship to it is also a major application of embodied meditation!

Working with the body's interaction with more "external" senses is excellent for life integration. Siight and sound tend to take much of our attention throughout the day.

True bottom-up embodied meditation

In some ways the culmination of practising many embodied meditation techniques and styles is simply to become spontaneous again.

Nearly all meditation techniques can be seen as "top-down", meaning they impose a form – usually a limitation of attention. A more free-feeling "bottom-up" approach is possible, where there is more of a "following" the body rather than leading it.

In this technique of (almost) no-technique you may flow between the techniques mentioned. You may move more than is typical in meditation, though often this is subtle (in conscious dance this subtle moving in response to the body is called the "small dance"). The method here is to listen and respond. It's more of a partner dance than a solo martial arts kata (form).

Key points:

- Listen
- Follow
- Stillness vs. "wiggle room"

- Responding to the body with kindness rather than reacting
- Being with discomfort if necessary/useful, AND be kind

Integration practices

In order to get the benefits of the core mediations "off the cushion" and into life, here are some variations that will help.

In the time of the Buddha, monks practised much more in nature, integrated socially by living with other monks, and did not have iPhones. So, modern context demands some innovation if we'd like to see a real transfer of these skills to daily life.

For more on this, see also the pit stops and informal practice ideas.

Eight embodied nature connections

While eco-embodiment is a whole field, the "big body" of nature should at least be considered in any book on the body and meditation.

Nature is your embodiment friend.

Put concisely, the natural world hugely supports our embodiment and we are not separate from it. The changing sensory stimuli (e.g., the wind, rain and sun on your skin) and the relaxing quality of nature really helps people stay present. We encourage you to meditate as often as you can in your garden, in parks or whenever you are out and about. In the time of the Buddha this was a given, which sadly has been lost in most modern retreats aiming for ease and efficiency.

In addition to the techniques already described here are some additional ones for nature connection:

Body awareness walk

Take a walk in nature[28]. Feel your body as you move through nature and notice how different environments affect your embodiment.

Breath swapping

Sit in a wooded area and visualise "swapping" breath with the plants while feeling the body. Scientifically, this is not far from the truth of O_2 and CO_2 exchange, of course.

Outside ground meditation

Lie on the ground. Perhaps on grass or somewhere similarly comfortable. Be aware of the touch of the earth and, if your mind drifts, bring your attention back to this touch.

Listen to nature

Sit or walk in nature and pay attention to the sounds you can hear and how it impacts your embodiment.

Fire watching

Watch a campfire and feel the warmth from it as you do so. Feel how it informs and relaxes your embodiment.

This is actually a surprisingly easy concentration meditation for most people. There's something about fire that's captivating.

Sea meditation

Stand in the sea and breathe in sync with the waves. Feel the water on your body and be present with the rhythm of the waves. Be aware

---

28 (of course, in a way, everything is "nature", but you get what we mean)

of your own fluid and its rhythmical nature while doing this. Rain or other bodies of water are useful if you live far from the sea.

Obviously only do this where it's safe! You can also do it next to the sea, simply by looking at it.

Tree Hugging/climbing

Touch the tree's bark, hug it if you like, and notice what that's like. Smell it. If a tree is safe to climb or sit in (at whatever height is safe for you), spend some time there. Tune into your senses and the sensations in your body.

Sun bathing meditation

The warm relaxing kiss of the sun on the skin can be a great meditation. Of course stay safe and use sun cream if you need to.

If you're drawn to this work, check out embodied eco-specialists like Charles Eisenstein, Philip Shepherd, Glen Mazis, Adrian Harris, Sarah Ryan and David Abram (to mention just six).

Five embodied relational meditations

Most meditation practice is solo, and while this is where it begins and is a foundation, we do live with others (unless we are hermits). The interpersonal context is worth doing some specific practice around if you want to see better transfer to this critical area of life. Sadly, many meditators get very good at being calm, focused and living on their own, but not with others! Yes, there will be some transfer across from your own solo practice to social application – essentially we practise relating to others with our relationship to ourselves – but this is sped up hugely by formal relational practise.

Here are a few techniques to bridge the gap between solo meditation and daily social life.

Coffee-shop practice

Take any small low-consequence purchase exchange that happens daily. For some this is buying a coffee (hence the name) or a newspaper, paying their bus fare to the driver, or anything similar that doesn't take long and is done fairly frequently. Instead of being on autopilot, really feel your body and pay attention to the server (you don't have to stare). Acknowledge their humanity and treat them as more than a delivery machine. Feel yourself with them. When you say, "thank you" or "goodbye", mean it and feel it. No need to be weird, but be very aware.

"How are you?" meditation

When people ask "how are you", use it as a reminder to really feel how you are. You may or may not choose to tell them, depending on what's appropriate socially, but FEEL how you actually are – even if you just say "OK" or "fine" for ease.

Equally, when you ask others how they are, actually ask. Be curious (but no need to push for a therapy session if they say "fine").

Influence walk

Go for a walk and as you pass people notice how you subtly influence them and how they influence you. For example, you may feel more open or closed towards another person, or you may feel an urge to move towards or away from them. You may become more or less like them as you observe them for a while, taking on or rejecting some of their embodiments.

NB: This can also reveal prejudices.

Dedicated partner practice

For this you need a willing partner as it involves sitting facing someone and being as present as you can to your experience with them and their experience with you. Taking turns to name sensations and emotions can be helpful, though you can do it silently. If you do talk, do not chat, but slloooowww down whatever you are saying. Use turn taking and timing. There are many possibilities and variations, but the key thing is to bring extra attention to what normally happens very quickly and unconsciously between us all.

A good place to start is to speak one sentence on a topic, wait for three breaths, and then speak again, and so on for the set time before swapping roles, with you both feeling your bodies as you do this. Alternatively, swap after each sentence, or add naming of sensations out loud, or observations of the other.

NB: Do not eye-gaze. Whilst this is a great practice it can lead to altered states that make feeling the body harder.

Bodywork practice

When receiving a massage or other bodywork, play attention and enjoy it as fully as you can. Notice your embodied responses to touch.

For more on relational practices, we recommend communities like Circling and Authentic Relating. There are some practices in traditional Buddhism where monastic living is a practice, but not as concentrated as these exercises.

A note on sexuality and sexual meditations

Sexuality is part of bodily life for most of us. Denial of, or repression and shame around sexuality is a significant part of how disembodiment happens for many. This can range from the harshly puritanical to the subtle ignoring of the genitals in many body-scan meditations!

Any embodied approach to meditation therefore must be "sex positive" in terms of not viewing sexuality itself as bad, nor seperating feeling sexuality from the human bodily experience, regardless of your boundaries around sexual activity and partners. Any approach to meditation that is anti-sexuality is by definition disembodying. One can embrace and enjoy embodied sexuality whether celibate, monogamous, in an open relationship with five consenting dolphins, or whatever. The key thing is being able to be present with sexuality as it arises in the body.

While there's a case to be made that ALL embodied meditations contain an element of sexuality, we have not included more explicitly solo or partner sexual meditations here. These can be very fruitful to explore, in an ethical, well-boundaried and trauma-aware way. We'd also offer some caution around much of modern neo-tantra[29], which often seems to be a "scene" where fantasy, drama, emotional bypassing and downright abuse appear fairly common. That being said, some great teachers and schools exist out there, but do explore with caution.

29 NB: neo-tantra has little or no connection with classical Buddhist tantra, which embraces all aspects of life but is not so focussed on sexuality.

Embodied Eating

What could be more bodily than food, eh? There are many traditions of mindful eating and while full silent presence to the experience of eating as per a Buddhist retreat can be great, there are other less demanding possibilities. Here are a few to explore:

Just Eat

Eat a meal without talking to anyone, watching TV etc. Give the tastes and smells and how your body is impacted by the food full attention.

Hunger and satisfaction meditation

Before eating a meal, notice how hungry you are. How do you know? How is it impacting you? Wait a few seconds before eating the meal while looking at it. Does craving come up? What are you doing with your body?

After you've finished eating your meal, notice how satisfied you are. How do you know? Are there different types of satisfaction (physical, emotional and in terms of pleasure for example?). Did you "overeat" – what does this mean? Were you confusing hunger with other needs that are still unmet (e.g. loneliness, relaxation, boredom etc)?

Drinking meditations

Take a drink of water and notice how far into the body you can feel it as you drink it. This type of "disappearance" meditation is excellent for literal deeper body awareness. Hot drinks can also provide micro-pleasure meditations throughout the day.

There is now a whole field of mindful eating and a related "no diet" movement that you can explore if these exercises build curiosity.

Tech Integration practices

When mindfulness was "invented", there was less technology. In many ways the phones and computers of today do not fundamentally change anything. Human nature is still the same. Yet, some adaptation techniques can be helpful to "bridge" into the virtual world. We are perhaps differently "wired" by this technology compared to our ancestors, and if nothing else it is a different type of context than the traditional practices were meant for.

Due to the attention-grabbing nature of technology, and especially apps that are DESIGNED for this, these practices can actually be quite difficult, and they should definitely be used as a supplement to more traditional practice rather than a substitute.

Note too that the less-ethical behaviour that often happens online in "flame wars", "trolling" and cyberbullying, is a result of the loss of empathy that happens during bodily dissociation. Sitting itself can be a somewhat numbing posture for many. Add to this the pull of stimulating visual input and information complexity, and you can see why it is advanced practice to stay with the body while online!

Given how much of modern life is in this technological context for so many, we actually find it astounding there are so few people teaching this integrative work. One reason few do is that tech-practice is often not a nice deep dive holiday into the body, but more a necessary challenge! Note that frequent little and occasional longer "detox" breaks can be helpful, but it is the integration that removes the need for these breaks and more fully improves our embodiment and lives.

Phone "grounding"

Feel your feet while talking on the phone or texting. Start with less interesting calls.

Breath texting

Take a full breath and feel your whole body between each sentence of a text message you are sending, or three full breaths before hitting send on any email or posting on social media. This can prevent a lot of trouble!

Computer body awareness – two ways

In order to maintain more body awareness while at a computer you can either try simultaneous or interruption methods.

The first method is to try and feel while online. If this is too challenging, you can be online but doing less-involved activity. Something like the visual and interpersonal stimulation of social media will be very difficult for most.

If this method is too difficult, or as an addition, you can set an alarm to go off and give you "windows" of body awareness throughout your tech use. These can be anywhere from a few seconds to a much longer period; whichever suits your life. You can also install software (e.g. RSI interruption software) to stop your devices so you HAVE TO stop using them. Drinking a lot of water will also force you to feel, move and take breaks!

Zoom empathy

If bored or in conflict on a video call, look at someone on the screen and connect empathically with them. Imagine how the place and time zone they are in is impacting them. How are they?

Coordination breaths

For work teams spread out globally, take three deep breaths together before a meeting to "sync". We use this a lot in team meetings at Embodiment Unlimited (the company where we both work).

This can also be done in person of course, I (Mark) regularly do a hugging version with my wife.

Facebook metta

Instead of visualising people and wishing them well, pull up their profiles on Facebook, Instagram or whatever! YouTube and comparative platforms can also be used to do a video version of this.

CLOSING COMMENTS ON ALL MEDITATIONS

Video support

Please note that we have made many of these meditations available on YouTube so you can do them as guided meditations to clarify the method clearer.[30] Embodied "transmission" works better through this medium too.

---

30 https://embodiedmeditationbook.com for links to everything, or https://www.youtube.com/c/Theembodimentchannel and https://www.youtube.com/c/KariYoga for guided embodied meditations.

"How" matters more than "what"

The manner in which you do the meditation IS what you are practising more than the actual technique. One definition of embodiment is simply "our how" and we become what we practise in this way.

The technique itself is not completely irrelevant, however, how you do it matters more for what you will be developing, and care should be taken here. Somewhat hilariously, I (Mark) did kindness meditation for about a year in a way that was borderline self-abusive. And I (Karin) have had students who were meditating or doing yoga to help them to cope with change more easily, practise at exactly the same time, in exactly the same place, doing exactly the same practice every day. Oooops.

The life application ladder again

For us "embodied meditation" does not only mean that you do a cover technique with the body, but that you take that embodiment into your life. This is the test of whether a practice is working for you. As well as formal practice please also consider informal practice and applications in regard to all these techniques.

If you are not getting life transfer fairly spontaneously after a few months, you may want to boost pit stops (Shinzen Young calls these "micro hits") and informal bridging practices. If a technique is ONLY practised formally on the cushion, it will likely stay there, and be of little use in real life.

A note on embodied ethics

Western approaches to meditation tend to focus on mindfulness techniques without focusing much on ethical practice. From a traditional point of view this misses a huge chunk of the practice, and is unwise. Meditation as an unethical mind is an agitated mind.

While it may seem old-fashioned or somehow "uncool", it is worth reviewing one's morality regularly. While I doubt many of you reading this are murdering anyone, we can all refine our ethics. Let's take theft for example. While it's likely that you're not stealing cars regularly, you may be padding your expenses account, taking small liberties, or even "stealing" time or energy from people who have not freely given it. Likewise, the positive side of generosity can also be a practice. In fact, in many Buddhist countries this is THE primarily practice for most people and not to be underestimated.

The body is also central to ethics, as our teacher Paul Linden has highlighted. We feel when we are going against our own values. It doesn't feel good. If you need a demonstration of this, imagine strangling to death a small fluffy kitten (or other cute animal you like) and notice what happens in the body. Very likely you contract, tense up, stop breathing, etc. We're WIRED for good, and the more embodied we become the more we can notice this.

This sense of a "kindness radar" can be refined with practice as we notice small ways we do harm day-to-day, and get better at tuning into things like life purpose that are about values too.

CHAPTER 4

CHALLENGES AND SUPPORTS

APPROACH TO POTENTIAL DIFFICULTIES

Paradoxically, in meditation we develop skills largely by NOT trying to change how we are. It is a confronting practice of awareness of what is. Having said that, as it also involves inclining towards kindness and working smartly, there are ways to intervene in your practice, guide yourself, and make some choices. Here are a few things to note to turn your practice into a skilful art:

Thoughts and distraction

If you are aware of doing lots of thinking, or that you are very distracted, that's okay. In fact, congratulations! Noticing these things is mindfulness in itself. When you notice you are lost in thought, you have already started to find yourself again. Bring yourself back to your body and continue. Practising mindfulness of the body is to some extent the practice of losing your body and coming back to it, over and over again.

While this is part of the practice, developing some concentration is enjoyable and the following may help:

- Guided meditations
- Changing when you practise (e.g. before you check email, or after exercise, or not midday)
- Altering where you practise
- Shifting techniques to a more active one, or taking a more active stance
- Reviewing your posture and making wise adjustments
- Noting, counting and/or labelling
- Spending more time in nature/reducing technology use
- Meditating with others
- Reviewing your general lifestyle and ethics

Note, many of these are solutions to many other meditation issues too

Pain (physical)

If you experience physical pain in your body, it can be helpful to focus on what emotions you can feel in your body, or which parts of your body feel OK or pleasurable.

If you are experiencing emotional pain, it can be helpful to notice how your physical body feels.

If focusing on your breathing creates anxiety, the full body scan may be a better practice for you right now.

You may initially think that the practice of awareness is making things worse, emotionally or physically, or you may notice a lot of thoughts. Part of this is simply that you are noticing more. You are no longer lost in distraction and you are now aware of what is going on.

Pain is magnified by overwhelm, our stress response to it, and our story about it. Most of what causes the *suffering* associated with pain[31], is how we react to it and what we tell ourselves about it. By reducing reactivity and getting very specific as to what pain is (where exactly? shape? type? etc), as well as stopping generating the story with bodily focus replacing mental chatter; suffering is often hugely reduced. In fact, modern mindfulness was born out of its efficacy in pain clinics.

While this "divide and conquer" method for pain is excellent, training oneself in the movement of attention away from the pain is also useful. You can take your attention to the extremities of your body, for example your hands or your feet, which tend to feel more neutral than your heart or abdomen where the stress responses are more noticeable and potentially intense. Or you can take your awareness to your sense of hearing or sight, being present with what is happening around you rather than inside you.

Human beings have this negativity bias that was mentioned earlier – the tendency to focus on what is wrong rather than on what is OK. This bias is created by your basic survival instincts and it can be a bit overactive. As neuropsychologist Rick Hanson famously said, "human beings' awareness is like Velcro for the negative things we experience, and Teflon for the positive. That's why it can help to guide your awareness to things that are not wrong, neutral or even pleasant to balance out that tendency to be preoccupied with difficulties experienced in life and during meditation.

Pain (emotional)/"overwhelm"

We simply cannot avoid some pain. We all get headaches, toothaches and heartaches. We tend to make it worse by overthinking, however. Thoughts about pain or problems can not only make them seem worse, but can also aggravate our nervous systems more than is necessary. Mindfulness can be a powerful tool to stop worrying and

---

31 Pain and suffering are not the same things, as many martial artists and BDSM practitioners
will tell you.

catastrophising – anticipating the worst possible scenarios, most of which will never come to pass. Coming back to the body and neutral physical sensations, or diverting attention away from catastrophising thoughts to our senses can interrupt these mental habits. Over time, this can also change the tendency to worry a lot – you may actually start to worry less and be more comfortable with the inevitable curveballs life throws at you.

This is the "divide and conquer" technique again.

Also, if you feel overwhelmed by what is going on inside you, remember you can always stop, move, do something else that is kind and nourishing, and try again another time or in another place. When I (Karin) was going through a major life transition and loss, I had already booked onto a long and intensive meditation retreat, only to find that my emotions were too strong to sit with. My teacher recommended sitting outside because being in nature with more space around me would give my emotions more space to dissipate. He recommended sitting on the beach looking at the horizon, which luckily I could do there. It really worked. If problems persist, do get advice from a qualified teacher. Also consider supplemental therapy or counselling. In our opinion psychotherapy and meditation are complementary but do not replace each other.

Trauma

Trauma is a huge field now and worth knowing the basics of as "stuff comes up" when meditating. Many people have had overwhelming experiences (a simple but good definition of trauma). Equally we can say that people who have become stuck in the fight-flight or freeze response (another simple trauma definition) will likely have challenges with this practice. Critically for many traumatised people the body is not a safe easy place to be, so care must be taken.

Let's start with some practical ideas if you think a trauma background may be impacting your meditation:

Some trauma-sensitive meditation ideas:

- Calibrate – i.e. meditate for less time, if for example sitting still or focussing on the body is too stressful[32]
- Use a lying down position if you are anxious
- Use a standing position if feeling powerless
- Note which meditations are more resourcing and which are more triggering. While there may be healing in the triggering ones, take it easy!
- Focus on body areas less associated with any trauma during scans
- Go between awareness of sight or sound (e.g. a bell) and the body, "titrating" what can be an intense experience without losing mindfulness
- Pick your timing to sit well – a time of day you're likely to be calmer
- Sit with trusted friends
- Sit in a place where you feel safe
- Try meditating in nature – this can have a regulating effect on your nervous system
- Consider trauma therapy as an adjunct
- Remember everything is impermanent – "this too will pass"
- Familiarise yourself with David Treleaven's work (on trauma-sensitive mindfulness
- Metta is usually helpful
- Anything else which is kind

Note: most traditional meditation teachers don't know much about trauma yet, sadly.

On a personal note, we've both been there, and wish you well. Healing is possible and can be helped by meditation as well as helping meditation.

---

32 When I (Mark) taught meditation to soldiers in Sierra Leone I found one minute was enough at first. More would make them very agitated. We built up from this. Do not judge yourself for doing less than others. There is no heroism in self brutalisation.

Agitation and sleepiness

It is very normal to either feel a bit agitated or sleepy during meditation. There are three areas of adjustments that can help you with agitation and sleepiness during meditation:

- Posture
- Gaze
- Breath

Agitation might be a sense that it's not OK or useful to sit still and do nothing. If it goes into something more overwhelming, follow the guidance above. If it's simply hard to sit still, you're feeling a bit wired, jittery, or restless, then it can help to do a calming practice before you meditate. You might do some yoga or qigong. Or you might benefit from "burning off" some excess energy by going for a brisk walk or run first. It may also help to practise first thing in the morning, before looking at your phone and getting engaged with the external world and other people. It can help to close your eyes or lower your gaze to minimise distraction, to relax your body a bit, maybe even to practise lying down. Taking some slow out breaths can help you settle, as well as counting the breath for the first couple of minutes of a practice.

Sleepiness could of course mean you are tired or sleep-deprived, in which case, get more rest! Perhaps consider meditating at a different part of the day, for example not just after eating or in the evening. And sometimes sleepiness seems to come along for no apparent reason. Your mind might feel a bit dull, not very present. In that case you could sit a bit more upright or meditate standing up. Try meditating with your eyes open and your gaze a bit upwards instead of closed or with a downward gaze. You can also take some deeper breaths to wake yourself up.

See also the list from the distraction section.

SUPPORTS

The stance section of this book

Visualisations, sounding, touch and movement

We have mentioned these throughout. Feel free to be creative here if you are hitting a problem.

Use of EYP poses pre-sit

While beyond the scope of this short book we use a system called Embodied Yoga Principles to change our stance and help students. A simple example would be the EYP self-care pose prior to meditating on self-compassion. You'll find a lot of the poses online, linked at: **https://embodiedmeditationbook.com**.

Community

I (Mark) used to measure my brain waves every day using the Muse device (there are others like it). What I noticed was that the most concentrated states were not when I did a particular technique, or when I meditated a lot even, but when I was around other meditators. Communities of practice also make it easier for most people to commit to a regular practice, and to explore sitting in meditation for longer periods of time.

Do not underestimate the great support "friends on the path" are.

Nature

Just as we are "co-regulated" by a supportive community, we are also "eco-regulated" by being in the natural world. It can be profoundly helpful to sit in nature, amongst trees or with a view of the sky and the sea. In more traditional schools of meditation it was customary to practise outside a lot. You may not be able to go to a Himalayan cave, but you could sit by a window, sit and meditate in the park, meditate on the beach. When your head is very full or you have a lot of emotional stuff going on, being in nature with more space around you can give you a sense of more space inside you, as well as extra headspace to cope with whatever is going on. As ever, don't take our word for it, try it out for yourself.

The inspired guide

Everyone needs an Obi Wan[33] at least sometimes. When meditating, the tangible physical presence of a mentor or guide can be helpful.

Sometimes our guides are alive, sometimes dead, sometimes we've met them, sometimes we've only imagined them. They could be ancestors, real teachers, famous people, archetypes, animals, or strange characters who just seem to come to us.

I (Mark) might imagine my father's or aikido teacher's supportive hand on my back when I need stability. This is a very physical "imagining", not a mental fancy, and can have a huge impact on practice.

Play with this, be open-minded.

33 If you do not know who this is, please go and watch the original Star Wars NOW.

CHAPTER 5

OVER TO YOU

HOW TO CHOOSE A PRACTICE

So, given the many methods in this book, and myriad others out there in the spiritual supermarket of the 21st Century, what on earth should you actually do?!!

Well, whatever the hell you like really (see method one below). Still here's some guidance for what's within and beyond this book.

We'll also look at how to establish a regular practice, as frankly without guidance most people fail in this in the longer term, and this is what leads to real and lasting changes. In a way, the best practice is just the one you do . . . but let's get clever about that.

Method one - whatever

If something really appeals to you and you feel enthusiasm for it, go for it. Follow your bliss. That's it. All techniques get to the same place anyway so you might as well do one you like. Do what's fun and easy.

Discussion over.

But one little thing . . .

. . . do choose and actually commit rather than jumping around. You'll get better results taking one practice as your core one (though you can supplement) and sticking to it for at least a few months.

Similarly, a regular time and place (if not travelling) will better establish a habit (which means less effort) than just doing it when you feel like it.

Remembering what you love

Why do you want to meditate? How does this reason link to what actually matters to you? Get really clear and honest about this.

Remind yourself of this when you don't feel like meditating, as sometimes you won't. All "discipline" is, is remembering what you care about.

Method two – trial and better

It can be worth testing what techniques lead to the desired fruit. For us a technique should not only have a more or less consistent useful short-term state impact (most people feel reliably more relaxed after breath meditation for example, though some get anxious from it[34]), but also show up in your life, positively impacting all major areas. If people aren't giving unsolicited positive feedback that could relate to a method after a while, then question if it's working.

While opinions differ over necessary testing timeframes, it's never overnight. We suggest students commit to 2-3 months of a particular practice before evaluating it (this is long enough to change habits where there may have been initial resistance). Others tell me this is a lot. And The Dalai Lama says you should apparently review the efficacy of your practice every ten years!

---

34 Careful here though as a skill-building technique may not be easy or necessarily feel pleasant, at least at first.

Method three - what you actually need

While there's a lot of wisdom in methods one and two, the problem is that people tend to pick practices that suit them. So they favour things that feel easy. This often means that rather than following the deep wisdom of their bodily intuition, they simply deepen neurosis by getting even better at what they're already good at.

The alternative is to pick practices, and do them in such a way as to build skills and ways of being that you need. Are you a more angry person who needs extra metta, or an ADHD human squirrel who needs extra concentration? Should you be meditating in a very structured, consistent way to build that aspect of yourself, or a more free-flowing, creative way to build that instead? Remember: how you do it matters more than what you are doing.

In time one can recognise the difference between being "called to" a practice, which feels like a deep longing, versus simply the smell of your own brand that is just reinforcing an established habit.

The balancing act here is that if you go too much against your conditioning you will not continue, but if you go too much with it you will not develop. This also brings us to . . .

Stabilising versus challenging

When making decisions about any practice including the type of meditation or technique, posture and duration of meditation, please ask yourself:

1. Do I need support and/or stabilisation? (i.e. when you are under-resourced or overwhelmed in your life)
2. Do I want to learn something new which will be a bit of a stretch for me? Or even a strong challenge that I am up for!!!?

If you answer yes to the first question, you need to build or protect your energy reserves. Learning something new will need a bit more effort and will likely drain you. Although it is not always quite as cut and dry as this (e.g. rest techniques can be inspiring), this is a good reflection to make sure you're being kind and developing your practice. In a nutshell: don't brutalise yourself and don't be complacent.

If you are overwhelmed with the circumstances of your life now, or you are new to meditation, choose what is easier and feels more resourcing for you. If it feels too difficult and you are struggling, this could put you off the practice. Calibration is key for beginners. Remember to find guidance from a qualified teacher if you are a complete novice, especially if you have mental health issues or have recently experienced a life-changing event. It may not be the right time to embark on a practice until you have managed to somewhat stabilise yourself.

If you are experienced and feel well-resourced you might choose to explore the edges of your comfort zone and expand them. For example, extend the length of your practice, so you have time to go into the fine detail of your body. In the body scan you could go so slowly, spending several minutes to bring awareness to each toe, and so on. Try different postures. Meditate with your eyes open if you normally have them closed. Make choices that help you develop your practice rather than coasting along in the same old way. This may mean you choose to practise things that you don't like and that are a little uncomfortable (but NOT if you are under-resourced).

Alongside the technique, there is also HOW you are practising – the attitude you bring to your awareness. Remember to practise at the very least being polite towards what you find in your body! The idea is that you're not dispassionately observing but that you are witnessing what is going on in your body with curious, kind interest. And please don't look at your breath or body as if you've just been shown a parking ticket! We're always balancing non-attachment with care.

You can mix it up a little and engage in different techniques and practices, for example explore some metta (loving kindness) meditation if you are under-resourced or struggling in a relationship, or a death meditation if you are not sure about your purpose in life (NOT for anyone who is depressed or anxious, or anyone who has suffered a recent bereavement).

And if you want to really develop your practice, pick ONE and stick to it for a few weeks or months to "dig a single deep well" and get to the water, rather than digging many shallow wells and never finding water. If you get bored with doing the same practice repeatedly, notice what the state of boredom feels like in your body. Maybe you are aware of patterns of not sticking with things in other areas of your life and how it might benefit you to practise something for a longer period of time. Cultivate what in Zen practice is called the "beginner's mind" – the capacity to be really present with how something is in the moment, as if you have never encountered it before. This also counteracts the common human tendency to be on autopilot much of the time. When you are stuck in autopilot, life is passing you by and you might miss out on a lot of things – to your detriment and even at your peril. We could compare this to spending a lot of time with your head in the virtual world of your smartphone, addicted to the distraction and entertainment it offers, whilst completely unaware of the world and people around you (and the car coming towards you as you step into the road!).

Length and regularity of practice

It's recommended to start with at least 10 mins a day to get the benefit, and to gradually extend that to 1-2 hours a day (in one or two sittings). After 8-10 minutes there is a "settling" – a reduction of stress hormones in the body that feels pleasant for many people. If you only have one minute, sit for one minute though. Quality is more important than quantity, as well as integration.

Practising at least 5-6 days a week helps to establish regular practice and habit. AND it's totally OK and even useful to have a day off. If we don't meditate every single day, we can notice the difference and not become too attached to the routine.

What if you miss a day you had planned to practise on? Remember to be kind to yourself. A good way is to celebrate and appreciate yourself when you have done your meditation, and to forgive yourself if you haven't. And renew your intention to practise tomorrow.

You may find a strange resistance to practice sometimes, with procrastination and excuses. Simply notice this and recommit. Sometimes watching a few talks, reading a book like this one ;-) or meditating with a friend can "get us back on the wagon". Often "resistance" is a sign we have pushed too hard or lost track of our motivation.

Practice "bookending"

It is helpful to incorporate these five elements when you **start** each practice:

1. Intention setting – be clear as to the purpose of the meditation (how will it benefit you and as a result other people in your life)
2. Commit to the duration of your practice and technique you're going to practise
3. Congratulate yourself for doing the hardest part (starting this practice)
4. Choose the best posture for your state right now and how you'd like to be (awareness and choice)
5. Begin with a gesture or small ritual of your choice (e.g. bringing your palms together, lighting a candle, etc)

And these six things to **end** each practice:

1. Notice the benefits (please note skill building isn't always fun straight away and benefits may only become noticeable after a while. Keeping a practice journal may help. More times than not you will feel good, and it is worth noting this to reinforce the practice)

2. Thank yourself for putting the effort in (not the outcome)
3. Set an intention to carry your mindfulness into your day
4. Set an intention to benefit others with your capacity to be mindful and embodied
5. Gratitude (thanking yourself for practising and appreciating the benefits for example) is a useful component of developing motivation to practise as well as a good antidote to the negativity bias
6. Conclude with a gesture or small ritual of your choice (e.g., bringing your palms together, blowing out a candle)

How to combine practices

For beginners it's best to stick to one technique, rather than swap around. With time you may start to combine techniques skilfully.

Many people find it helpful to start with a simple body scan – to become more body aware – before another practice. This can also help with emotional digestion which may be the first 10 minutes of any sit. Others establish concentration with a breath focus (even the tip-of-the-nose kind we usually don't recommend) and then move on. Some finish with metta which may feel like a relational "extension" of what comes before. A completely fluid intuitive "no method" approach is also possible. Metta can be used to gain courage for a hard practice, or as a nice ending to one.

We encourage you to experiment with order and mixing meditation "cocktails".

Tips to establish a regular practice

• Reflect deeply on how meditation will benefit the things in your life that you care about (e.g. kids, work, sex life). "Play forward" negative things happening now that meditation could prevent/reduce. Motivate yourself with your actual values

- Meditate at the same time every day (mornings, before getting involved with daily life, work well for most people, while evenings are great for others). Experiment before picking a time and sticking to it
- Stick to a place in your house if you can and make it neat and pleasant
- Don't turn your phone or computer on first! An alarm clock will help if you normally use your phone to set a timer
- Practise with others – regularly sit with a group or find a meditation buddy
- Accountability – if you have a buddy or a teacher you can ask them to hold you accountable for practising regularly
- Keep a practice journal to make a note of the benefits you are noticing as a result of meditation – this will motivate you to keep going

Top tips for complete beginners

- Remember, you will notice thoughts and do not need to "empty your mind"!. If it seems your head is "busy" and full of things, this is normal but gets easier for most with time
- Getting distracted is normal, keep coming back to the body and thank yourself for noticing when you do (don't blame yourself!)
- Guided meditations may be easier to focus on (e.g. on an app, some are recommended later)
- Breath counting can also be helpful for focus
- Little and often is better than pushing too much at first
- Sit in a chair if you like. It's not more spiritual to have painful knees or to sit on the floor
- Do whichever technique you enjoy most (experiment with a few first). The pleasure meditation may be especially helpful to condition yourself!
- Groups and buddies, as mentioned above
- Tell everyone you're doing it, especially about the benefits

- Take the practice seriously, don't take yourself seriously
- Commit to 4-6 times a week, for ten minutes, for two months – only then decide if it is for you or not. Well done for giving it a go!

Top tips if you had a practice but you dropped it

- Remind yourself of your reasons for starting and see if they still hold true. You may need a new reason to begin again
- MAKE time, you are not too busy to prioritise ten minutes for something you know will help almost everything else
- Adjust your life so you are not stressed or exhausted all the time (doh!)
- Try different techniques (especially if you got bored)
- Listen to a few talks from inspiring teachers
- Book yourself on a meditation course or retreat to deepen and support your practice
- Just "get back on the horse" (and don't beat yourself up about getting off it)

Reflections for people who have been sitting for more than ten years

- Is your goal and motivation still clear or are you on "autopilot"?
- Check your method is optimised for your goal
- Are you overly attached to one style/teacher or under-committed, jumping around to whatever is convenient and "shiny"?
- Reflect on the benefits of your practice and get feedback as to whether it has changed you
- Do you have a community of support and accountability? Could you be kidding yourself about your practice and what you need to develop without one?
- If you have "plateaued", what is needed?

- Have you developed an unhelpful "spiritual identity" or smug superiority around being a meditator?
- Still got a sense of humour around it?

Making your commitment

Now the most important part in the whole book. Making a firm commitment to getting on your arse (or feet, or back).

Write below what you WILL do: 4-6 days a week, 10min +, with a concrete technique, and how you will remember to do it. Write your real motivation for doing it. Give a definite time and place to do it, and decide how you will overcome likely challenges that may arise. Find a pen, write on this book, put reminders in your diary, or similar. Tell you friends about your plans and commit publicly in other ways – for example on social media if you wish.

If you would like to experiment with the various techniques, that's fine. Make a commitment to how you will do that and within what time frame; and then a commitment to pick one technique and deepen your practice of that.

CHAPTER 6

CONCLUSION AND RESOURCES

KEY POINTS - REVIEW

Before you put this book down and write us a five-star review on Amazon . . . or pass it on to a friend who can't afford to buy it (both would be appreciated), make sure you've gotten the best from it:

Actually meditate

While many techniques are presented in this book, the main takeaway is to meditate. Practise!

Learn to meditate AS a body, not just ON the body

The next key lesson is to meditate AS a body, not just ON the body. Again, this may take a little while to get.

Aspects of the skill of body awareness

The practices in this book will help you build these four aspects of embodied awareness:

1. More detail
2. More depth
3. More fully
4. More of the time

Safety versus learning choice

When you can, pick what you need to learn rather than what is easy, pick what is easy/supportive over what you need to grow long-term if you are currently overwhelmed.

Core embodied meditation techniques

Make sure you fully explore these two:

- Body scan
- Breath awareness

Postures

Try meditating in all of these:

- Sitting
- Standing
- Lying down
- Walking

Frames and perspectives

- Close and connected (versus far)
- Embracing and warmly involved rather than coldly observing
- Aware with a "womb-like" attention (an instruction derived from Buddhist texts)
- Intimate with, not separate from, the body
- Practising being really welcoming to what you notice

What's not embodied meditation (as we would define it)

- Anything unkind. While some effort and even moderate non-damaging physical discomfort and non-overwhelming emotional challenge may be useful, the basic rule is: **If it ain't kind, it ain't meditation**
- Disembodied visualisation, ritual or mantra

Suggested contexts to transfer your embodied awareness into

- The natural world
- Eating and drinking
- Interpersonal relationships of all kinds (family, work, sex, etc.)
- Technology use

RECOMMENDED RESOURCES FOR FURTHER STUDY

There's a lot of good stuff out there now, and it is much more easily accessible online than it ever has been before. We are, in fact, very lucky to live in these times.

Traditions

We are aware that people may already be practising within one of the classical traditions or may want to explore these. Within all major traditions there exist both "pro" and "anti" body trends, so here are a few recommendations for the former. There are many more good teachers, but these we can recommend personally.

> Theravada – The Forest Sangha Tradition
> Western Insight – Tara Brach, Jack Kornfield, Sharon Salzberg, Shinzen Young, Jon Kabat-Zin, Rick Hanson and Joseph Goldstein are all legends
> Zen – Hallow Bones Sangha, Plum Village and Dianne Hamilton
> Tibetan Buddhist – The Dalai Lama, Pema Chödrön, Mingyur Rinpoche, Tsoknyi Rinpoche
> Traditional (not "neo") tantric meditation – Christopher Wallis

Modern movements:

> Integral – Miles Kessler (Israel based/online), Ken Wilber (USA)
> Somatic movement influenced – Jamie McHugh
> Hardcore Dharma – Daniel Ingram

Retreat Centres

The Moulin de Chaves (Martin and Gail Aylward + friends – France), Gaia House (UK), and Insight Meditation Society (USA) are solid places for practice generally.

While an excellent and affordable option for intermediate to advanced practitioners, we do NOT recommend "Goenka-style" vipassana retreats for beginners. We are aware of many people having mental and physical problems as a result of the very intense schedules adhered to on these retreats.

We are also cautious of some US centres that have adopted a radical identity politics/ critical theory ideology in recent years.

Further reading

The Body – Paramananda – clear, short and "light". We recommend this book to complete beginners, though it is worthwhile reading for all levels.

Martin Aylward's upcoming book *Awake Where You Are* is excellent for more depth, and would be a good addition to this book.

We also recommended *The Science of Enlightenment* by Shinzen Young, Christopher Wallis' *Tantra Illuminated*, *Loving Kindness – The Revolutionary Art of Happiness* by Sharon Salzberg, *Seeing That Frees* by Rob Burbea, anything by Judith Blackstone, Thich Nhat Hanh, Ken Wilber (theory), Ken McCleod (deep), Jon Kabat-Zinn (scientific/ secular), Rick Hanson (scientific/secular), Pema Chödrön (heart-led), Daniel Ingram (for stages of enlightenment), The Dalai Lama (Tibetan Buddhism), Noah Levine (punk rock Buddhist alternative!), David Treleaven (trauma-sensitive mindfulness) and Philip Shepherd (nature connection). For a very good easy to read introduction to trauma we recommend Steve Haines' *Trauma Is Really Strange*.

Podcasts

The Embodied Facilitation Podcast
Embodied Yoga and Meditation Podcast

Technology

Good **meditation apps** include *Brightmind* (our favourite), *Buddhify* and *Insight Timer*, though there are many others. *State* is also excellent for breathwork.

We have had some fun with the brainwave-measuring device Muse and other **bio-feedback technology**, but the danger is relying on them and not your own somatic sense.

KEEPING IN TOUCH

If you'd like to keep in touch with us the best way is to **get the regular Embodiment Unlimited newsletter**. Go to: https://embodiedmeditationbook.com and you'll find a bunch of free offers too.

Meeting up

We also often meet students in real life for coffee and group dinners on our travels. Simply drop us an email replying to the newsletter if you see we're in your area.

Social Media

If you really want to reach enlightenment, follow us and accumulate good merit in all five realms:

- Mark's Instagram – @warkmalsh
- Karin's Instagram – @yoginikari108
- Karin's Facebook/LinkedIn – search: Karin van Maanen
- You can find us both at the Embodiment Unlimited social media accounts and connect with others who liked this book there
- Mark's Facebook . . . is not for the easily offended . . . (likely banned by now actually)
- YouTube – search "embodied meditation" and we come up
- Or find links to all the above at: https://embodiedmeditationbook. com

A FINAL BLUNT NOTE

If what is in this book has not shown up significantly in your everyday life by now – money, work, sex, parenting, etc. – then you've not yet understood what it offers. Practise what's in the book, and then read it again to experience how your embodied and experiential understanding can develop.

Please find ways to enjoy your meditation. This is mandatory.

Also, if meditation makes you feel good, but does not motivate you nor better enable you to contribute positively to the world . . . you've been doing it wrong. Start again.

. . . and a nice one

Lastly, well done for getting this far. Seriously, it's a big deal to make the effort with this stuff. Well done. The body is an adventure, a celebration, a homecoming, a portal, a profound journey, and a fiesta. Welcome to the party.

Printed in Great Britain
by Amazon

70805157R00081